ADD in the Workplace

Choices, Changes, and Challenges

Kathleen G. Nadeau, Ph.D.

Brunner-Routledge
New York & London

Library of Congress Cataloging-in-Publication Data

Nadeau, Kathleen G.
    ADD in the workplace : choices, changes, and challenges / Kathleen
G. Nadeau.
        p.   cm.
    Includes bibliographical references and index.
    ISBN 0-87630-847-7 (pbk.)
    1. Vocational guidance.   2. Attention-deficit disordered adults-
-Employment.   3. Attention-deficit hyperactivity disorder.
I. Title.
HF5381.N215   1997   97-1312
331.5'94—dc21   CIP

Copyright ©1997 by Kathleen G. Nadeau

Published by
Brunner-Routledge
29 West 35th Street
New York, NY 10001

Manufactured in the United States of America
10   9   8   7   6   5

I would like to express my appreciation to all the adults with Attention Deficit Disorder who have worked with me over the past years. You have taught me much, and together we have learned even more about how to understand, to manage, and even to celebrate living with ADD. This book was written to pass on this knowledge so that other adults with ADD will have a better chance to transform their lives into a success story, as so many of you have done. With admiration for your perseverance and for your pioneering efforts, I dedicate this book to all of you.

Contents

Acknowledgments

I want to acknowledge so many of the people with whom I have worked over the past several years in the growing field of adult Attention Deficit Disorder. The sudden explosion of awareness of ADD in adults has made this a very interesting and exciting time. One of the most appealing aspects of working in the field of adult ADD is the atmosphere of sharing, mutual interest, and mutual support.

I want to thank Paul Jaffe, who has been a real pioneer in fighting for the recognition of ADD in adults. His publication, *ADDendum*, has covered issues of adults with ADD from the very beginning and has always been of the highest quality. He has served well as historian, reporter, and gadfly, a true activist working to keep the needs of adults with ADD in the public eye.

I want to thank Mary Richard, who has taught me a great deal about educational issues for adults with ADD. She worked diligently within Children and Adults with Attention Deficit Disorder (CH.A.D.D.) as chairperson of the Adult Issues Committee; now, as president of this organization, she is putting the issues of adults with ADD on the front burner. My appreciation is also extended to John Ratey, Andrea Miller, and Sari Solden for sharing with me their experiences and ideas about women with ADD; it has been a privilege working with them to increase awareness of women's issues, which have been long overlooked.

Nancy Ratey has been a wonderful, sharing, and enthusiastic partner in considering workplace issues. Her experience in coaching adults with ADD in the workplace is invaluable, and she has been unstinting in sharing her time and knowledge with me. My thanks also to Pat and Peter Latham, who edited the first book on workplace issues for adults with ADD and with whom I have continued to work on a wide range of projects. As pioneers in the field of workplace issues and as cofounders of the National Center for Law and Learning Disabilities, they bring a wealth of legal knowledge as well as an in-depth clinical understanding of ADD and learning disabilities.

Patricia Quinn has proved to be a wonderfully stimulating friend and colleague. Her counsel, beginning with the first book on ADD for children, has been invaluable.

To all of you, and to others too numerous to mention, I want to both recognize your contributions and thank you for your support in the creation of this book.

IN THIS CHAPTER

This chapter provides a brief description of the "ADD-friendly" style and format of the book and addresses such general questions: Why are we suddenly talking about ADD? Is ADD just a fad or a genuine biological disorder?

1

ADD in the Workplace: An Overview

Why a Book on ADD in the Workplace?

As children with Attention Deficit Disorder (ADD) mature and leave their school years behind, the workplace rather than the classroom becomes their greatest challenge. An enormous amount has been written about how to help children with ADD function better in the classroom but very little attention has been given to how ADD symptoms affect work life.

Many of the things we do at work require skills taught during our school years. At work most of us must read, write, make calculations, organize and carry out projects, meet deadlines, learn new information, and pay attention during meetings and lectures. This book has been written to respond to the needs of people with ADD after they have shifted from classroom to career. To help them understand their disorder, to help them advocate for themselves at work, to inform them about accommodations that may benefit them at work, and to teach them techniques to better manage ADD symptoms that detract from their workplace performance and how to choose or create an ADD-friendly work environment. Most importantly, this book is written to increase their odds of making a good "ADD-wise" career choice, one that is based on self-knowledge, on an understanding of ADD.

About This Book

This book is an attempt to organize and integrate what I have learned over the past decade while treating adults with ADD who have struggled with career and workplace difficulties. What you will read here is based on my clinical experience. The process of learning about adults with ADD—their patterns, struggles, and successes—has been one of mutual discovery for my clients and me. Some of my clients have achieved remarkable career success despite their struggles with ADD and other types of learning difficulties. Although most did not apply the ADD label to their struggles over the years, they were aware of difficulties with attention, memory, and organization, and many of them developed ingenious and effective means of coping with their ADD. Their self-observations, their perspective on career success and failure, and the techniques they developed to cope with frustrating ADD symptoms have been included in this book.

While this book was written for adults with ADD, it should be useful for friends, relatives, employers, coworkers and career counselors as well.

As is so often the case, clinical experience precedes research. It is my hope that this book, which is based on my own experience and, where cited, on the experience and observations of others, will not only prove useful to adults struggling with ADD symptoms at work but will also spark an interest among social scientists to conduct research that will investigate and refine the approaches outlined here.

How to Read This Book

Adults with ADD often report difficulty in maintaining their focus long enough to read an entire book. If this is true for you, don't worry. You shouldn't feel obliged to march straight through it from beginning to end. Depending upon your circumstances, you may not choose to read every chapter. By reading the descriptive synopsis at the beginning of each chapter you can quickly decide whether to continue or to move on to a topic more relevant to you.

The Format

This book is designed to be "ADD-friendly"; that is, it is readable and engaging, and the material is presented in "digestible bites" suitable for people who have difficulty concentrating. Even people without concentration problems will appreciate the book's convenient format.

This book's ADD-friendly features include:

- A descriptive synopsis at the beginning of each chapter
- Clear headers that allow you to scan quickly to find sections that interest you
- Open space to reduce eyestrain
- Visual stimulation through good graphic design, variation in font style and size, and illustrations
- A clear, succinct, and interest-grabbing writing style
- A differentiation between straightforward information and illustrative personal stories
- Memorable aphorisms that sum up important ideas

"ADD-Friendly"
=
"User-Friendly"

The Aphorisms

Benjamin Franklin was a master of aphorisms and used many in *Poor Richard's Almanack*:[1]

A stitch in time saves nine.

Never put off until tomorrow what you can do today.

Early to bed and early to rise makes a man healthy, wealthy, and wise.

There are some ADD experts who even suggest that Benjamin Franklin was an adult with ADD who developed effective tools for memory and organization as ways to compensate for his ADD symptoms![2] As you can see, many of his best-known sayings relate directly to difficulties experienced by most adults with ADD.

Following Ben Franklin's example, you will find summary statements throughout this book that are brief and easy to remember, such as these:

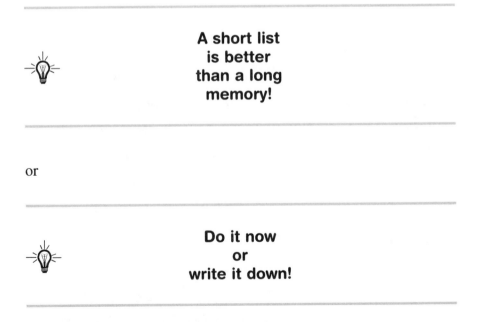

**A short list
is better
than a long
memory!**

or

**Do it now
or
write it down!**

These brief statements are an ADD-friendly memory tool to help you remember the essence of what has been described at length.

Why is ADD Suddenly Receiving So Much Notice?

A DD is a very common disorder, one that has always been with us but that has now become better recognized and understood, thanks to the writing and research of a small group of social scientists and psychotherapists. The first ADD self-help organization, Children with Attention Deficit Disorder (CH.A.D.D.),[3] has grown from a small grassroots organization to an international enterprise in only a few short years. While the organization was originally focused on children with ADD, it has now officially changed its name to include the word *adults* in response to recent awareness that ADD affects people of all ages. The demand for services for adults has grown so rapidly that another national organization, the National Attention Deficit Disorder Association (ADDA),[4] has changed its charter to focus exclusively on meeting the needs of adults and families.

Many forces have combined to bring ADD into the spotlight in the United States today. Let's take a look at what some of those forces may be.

Advances in Neuroscience

With rapid advances in psychopharmacology and in the technology of neuroscience, we are suddenly able to measure and better understand the neurological processes of people with ADD.[5] Just a few short years ago, experts in the field believed that ADD only affected children,[6] that most were boys, and that they outgrew ADD during adolescence. We now know that ADD affects both males and females and that those with ADD are affected to varying degrees throughout their lifetime.[7] New noninvasive techniques such as PET scans and SPECT scans allow researchers to measure and understand brain differences between those with ADD and those unaffected by ADD.

Public Mandates

The ADD movement was started by parents of children with ADD. One of the reasons that ADD is on the front burner now is that the efforts of this movement have resulted in public mandates that require certain types of organizations (in academic and employment settings) to accommodate people with ADD. The Individuals with Disabilities Education Act (IDEA)[8] requires schools to provide appropriate services and accommodations to children with disabilities (including ADD).

With the passage of the Americans with Disabilities Act (ADA),[9] adults with ADD have opportunities similar to those of children. Now that we understand much more about how to help individuals with ADD and have passed legal mandates to assist both children and adults with ADD, there is a strong incentive for those with the disorder, who have always been with us, to be diagnosed and to receive treatment.

Social Forces

In this century—and even more so in this generation—our society has undergone radical changes; these have created social conditions that may make ADD symptoms more intense. One way of thinking of this is that society is less ADD-friendly today than in previous times. (You'll hear more about this concept of an ADD-friendly culture in Chapter 9, as I discuss what forces can make a work environment ADD-friendly or ADD-unfriendly.) Societal changes that may worsen ADD symptoms include:

Sedentary Work with Prolonged Mental Concentration

Some experts in the field have suggested that ADD appears to be a more prevalent problem today because jobs are more likely to be sedentary and require long periods of concentration.[10] In the past, jobs more often involved active, hands-on activity, which is more suitable for some people with ADD. Thom Hartmann, an adult with ADD and widely recognized writer on ADD topics, suggests that the condition of ADD, which we now define as a neurological disorder, is actually a set of traits that were highly adaptive in earlier times but are less suited to today's world.[11]

The Electronic World of Instant Gratification

Over the past two generations we have moved away from activities that train the brain to focus, follow through, and remember. Memorization at school has been deemphasized, and reading has become a rare recreational activity for children. Children in the past two generations have grown up in a world of television, fast action, and sound bites. Communication is casual and oral. Our computers and voice mail remember for us. Children accustomed to rapid-paced visual stimulation and to largely oral communication are poorly prepared for workplace activities requiring sustained focus, attention to detail, and long-term planning.

Divorce and Single Parenting

Yet another huge change affecting children over the past two generations has been the rising divorce rate. Children with ADD need a tremendous amount of structure, regularity, and support at home. The circumstances created by divorce provide a virtual recipe for increasing the symptoms of ADD. Raising a child with ADD can be a daunting task even for parents who are happily married and who work together to develop ADD parenting skills. It is less likely that divorced parents of an ADD child can work together cooperatively for the benefit of their child. Divorced parents may even blame one another for causing the child's ADD symptoms rather than coordinate their efforts to help reduce their child's troublesome ADD behaviors.[12]

The Stresses in Dual-Career Families

Even in intact families there are forces at work in contemporary life that may increase the intensity of ADD symptoms in both children and adults. Both parents in a dual-career family often have long commutes and long work hours with little time and energy remaining to create a predictable, supportive, structured home life. The lives of children have become more stressed and activity oriented at least partially in response to the need of working parents to have their children supervised for 10 or more hours each day. Both children and adults with ADD respond best to low stress, low pressure, flexibility, and stability. Unfortunately, our contemporary lives provide just the opposite of these.

Speculations and Reality

Although we can only speculate as to whether these societal and cultural influences have converged to intensify ADD symptoms or to make them more prevalent, both conclusions seem reasonable. What is clear, however, is that we now have a better understanding of ADD and how to treat it. And we now have laws, covering both children and adults, that require schools and employers, among others, to respond to the needs of those with ADD.

How Common Is ADD?

The behaviors related to ADD are among the most common reasons children are referred for psychological treatment. Some experts estimate that 1 in every 15 to 20 children has a significant level of ADD.[13] The prevalence of ADD in adults has not yet been adequately studied, but recent estimates suggest that between 6 and 10% of the adult population have Attention Deficit Hyperactivity Disorder (ADHD).[14] Because these estimates were made before widespread recognition of females with ADD and of nonhyperactive ADD, it is possible that the real incidence of ADD is higher. While there are those who believe that the majority of children with ADD outgrow their symptoms, most professionals in the field are now convinced that to some extent ADD is a lifelong condition for the majority of those who are affected.[15]

Is ADD Just the Latest Fad?

ADD has received a great deal of media attention recently, leading many to respond with skepticism to this "disorder of the '90s." In fact, some critics have charged that ADD is a fad, the behavioral equivalent of a "flavor of the month."[16] Just as with any recently understood, highly publicized disorder, there are inevitably many people who incorrectly use ADD as a self-diagnosis and many undertrained professionals who misdiagnose ADD in their clients. Furthermore, among adults suffering from a wide range of disorders there are those who seek an ADD diagnosis because it seems to them to be a more socially acceptable, benign label. In this sense, ADD has become a fad.

On the other hand, ADD is a genuine neurobiological disorder, one that, if untreated, can cause enormous difficulty and suffering in the lives of those who have it. ADD is a condition that deserves careful diagnosis by a trained professional, a diagnosis that should only be made if symptoms have a long-term, significant effect on the functioning of an individual. Those of us who work in the field welcome the efforts toward much-needed public education about this disorder that affects so many people, but we deplore media coverage that trivializes, misrepresents, or sensationalizes it.

The Struggle to Receive Acceptance and Understanding

In the work-obsessed American culture, the recent publicity about ADD seems to have sparked a debate that places two strongly held attitudes at odds with one another.

The "Just Do It!" School of Thought

Because hard work and self-discipline are values so engrained in our American culture, it is easy for some to condemn those with ADD as lazy, morally inferior, or excuse seeking.[17] We in this "land of the free and home of the brave" like to believe that individuals have the capacity to exert full control over their actions and reactions. This approach to life might be described as the "Just do it!" school of thought. It's very tempting to believe that life can be that simple, that if we just try hard enough we can conquer anything.

Scientific Understanding of Behavior

Equally strong, however, is our belief in science and technology. As we lead the world in medical research, we Americans take great pride in our increasing understanding of neuroscience. With our more sophisticated understanding of brain processes, we are moving away from a simplistic, moralistic approach toward behavior and toward an enlightened, scientific-treatment-oriented approach.

If we look at ADD in the light of our growing understanding of the neurochemistry and neurophysiology underlying ADD, it becomes difficult for us to cling to the "Just do it!" school of thought. Neuroscience is gradually unveiling the complexities of the brain, demonstrating that who we are is profoundly influenced, even controlled, by brain structure and brain chemistry.

**An ADD
diagnosis is an
explanation,
NOT
an excuse.**

The risk in understanding ADD as a neurological disorder is to overemphasize that ADD symptoms are not the fault of the individual and to underemphasize the individual's responsibility to manage the disorder. Some adults with ADD have taken the position that others should tolerate their problem behaviors, that professionals have the responsibility to find and offer solutions, and that employers must accommodate them have done a great disservice to the ADD community. This passive victim's approach to disability has contributed to an ADD backlash in which writers in some popular magazines have decried ADD as a scam and as a refuge for the lazy and incompetent.[18] The Americans with Disabilities Act doesn't relieve adults with ADD of responsibility for taking charge of their disability; it only attempts to describe a limited but important role that employers can play in supporting them in the workplace (for more information about the Americans with Disabilities Act, see Chapter 14). A diagnosis of ADD doesn't divest people of responsibility for the difficulties they experience with their family members, friends, and coworkers; it only provides a framework for understanding and learning to manage this challenging disability.

Taking Charge of ADD

The key to effectively dealing with ADD is to find the middle ground between the "Just do it!" and "It's not my fault" approaches. The healthiest attitude toward attention deficit disorder can be summed up in this phrase:

**Take charge of
your ADD,
or it will
take charge of you!**

How can you take charge? You can do the following:

 Educate yourself as much as possible about ADD.

❷ Make an accurate ADD self-assessment.

❸ Seek appropriate help for your ADD.

❹ Learn techniques to minimize your ADD symptoms.

5 Recognize and use your positive traits.

6 Make the most informed and appropriate career choice or change.

7 Learn ways to make your job more "ADD-friendly."

8 Learn how to appropriately advocate for yourself at work.

This book is designed to help you learn how to take charge of your ADD at work so that you can focus all of your energies on building a successful and satisfying career.

This chapter discusses how an ADD workplace evaluation should go beyond a basic diagnosis to address specific workplace issues, career choices and changes, and workplace accomodations.

Seeking an Adult ADD Workplace/Career Assessment

A "standard" diagnostic evaluation of ADD in adults is designed to investigate whether you have symptoms that indicate the presence of ADD, and to assess other conditions which may coexist with ADD. Normally this type of basic diagnostic evaluation barely touches on career concerns. If your primary concerns are related to the workplace you will need to consider your ADD in a more specialized way.

How Do I Find Someone to Evaluate ADD Workplace Issues?

It can be very difficult to find an ADD specialist who is well versed in ADD career issues or to find a career counselor knowledgeable about the needs of adults with ADD. You may find that you need to work simultaneously with both an ADD specialist and a career counselor in order to really address the whole range of pertinent issues. In selecting an ADD specialist you may want to ask the following questions:

 How much of your practice consists of working with *adults* who have ADD?

② Have you worked extensively on career issues with ADD adults?

③ Do you have experience with the Myers-Briggs Type Indicator and its use on career issues?

④ Would you feel comfortable working in tandem with a career counselor to help me address my career concerns?

An ADD Workplace Evaluation

This type of assessment is appropriate when your focus is on your current job. Many adults seek assessment when they have reached a crisis point at work. Their question is immediate, urgent, and practical: How can I improve performance in my current job so that I don't lose it? This type of workplace assessment should address the following:

▧ How your ADD specifically effects your job performance.

▧ Whether coexisting learning disabilities may impact performance.

▧ What coping strategies you should implement to take charge of ADD.

▧ What accommodations your employer could reasonably provide.

▧ What your personality type is, and how recommendations should be tailored to your personality in order to be most effective.

▧ What your employment history is, and what aspects of prior jobs have been positive or negative.

Let's consider each of these areas separately.

1. Evaluation of the Impact of ADD on Current Job Functioning

The Adult ADD Workplace Questionnaire, developed by the author (found in the Appendix) is an extensive list of questions designed to pinpoint exactly how ADD impacts your functioning in your particular job. This questionnaire was developed to help you and your career specialist evaluate the on-the-job impact of your ADD in a detailed and highly specific fashion. It is divided into categories in order to help you organize this self-assessment. It also can be very useful to obtain the feedback of a trusted friend or colleague in making this self-assessment. Those who work closely with you may have valuable input. Of course, you should only engage the assistance of someone else if you feel comfortable in sharing your workplace difficulties with him or her.

2. Evaluation of Coexisting Learning Problems

On the workplace questionnaire just described, there is a section titled "Other Cognitive Problems." If you answered "yes" to a number of these questions, you may be struggling with not only ADD, but also with learning disabilities. The tests appropriate for evaluating learning disabilities in adults will not be listed here because they need to be selected by a learning disabilities (LD) specialist. The type of testing that would be appropriate depends on the types of learning problems that are suspected.

The combination of LD with ADD is very common, although many adults were never evaluated for learning problems when they were children. Such learning problems, even in their mildest form, can cause significant problems for adults on the job.

You might ask, "Why bother about learning disabilities now? I'm already finished with school." The answer is that even when we are through with school we are *never* through with learning. To remain competitive and employable in today's high tech world we are constantly under pressure to learn new things.

Many areas of difficulty can be improved through remedial tutoring, even in adulthood. Testing for learning disabilities can help your ADD career professional guide you to a better job match or career choice.

3. Identification of Coping Strategies to Improve Performance

Chapters 3, 4, and 5 of this book have been written specifically to help you identify appropriate coping strategies.

4. Determination of Reasonable Accommodations from the Employer

To determine, with your counselor, which types of accommodations would be most helpful and appropriate for you, refer to Chapter 11, which lists a range of possible accommodations for ADD in the workplace. Be sure to read Chapter 14 on the Americans with Disabilities Act to be sure that your employer is required to provide accommodations and under what circumstances.

5. Identification of Personality Type and Recommendations

Your personality type is so important to making good career and workplace recommendations that Chapter 6 has been devoted to discussing personality types, as measured by the Myers-Briggs Type Indicator (MBTI), and how different personality types need different kinds of coping strategies and different ideal career matches. The MBTI is quick to take, usually inexpensive, and can provide extremely valuable information to help you assess what are your best workplace strategies.

6. Evaluation of Employment History

In order to evaluate your employment history from an ADD perspective you should go through an informal "job analysis" of each position you have held, including your current position. You will find a list of questions on page 17 to help you structure these job analyses. If you find this process too tedious or difficult to go through alone, it can

ADD Job Analysis

① What were the "pluses" in this job?

② What were the "minuses"?

(List anything you can think of in making each of these lists. Your list might include things such as pay, opportunity for advancement, my supervisor, my coworkers, commuting time, types of assigned tasks, variety, challenge, interest, general workplace environment, etc.)

③ What primary problems did I have when functioning in this job?

(a) Were these problems ADD-related?

(b) Were they problems I could reduce or eliminate by "taking charge" of my ADD, learning habits and coping skills?

(c) Were they problems that called for accommodations from my employer?

(d) Were they problems over which I had no influence or control?

④ How "ADD friendly" was my job?

Boss

Work assignments

Structure

Distractions

Repetition

Interest level

General atmosphere

Level of paperwork requirements

be done through a discussion of each position with your ADD career counselor.

7. Cognitive Functioning

The tools recommended in items 1–6 may need to be supplemented by the Wechsler Adult Intelligence Scale-Revised and the Wechsler Memory Scales-Revised if you have not already undergone neuro-psychological testing in obtaining your initial ADD diagnosis. These tests are very helpful in pinpointing both strengths and weaknesses across a wide range of cognitive skills, which are often called for in the workplace.

Can Your Current Job *Become* the "Right" Job for You?

If you are like a lot of people with ADD, your first instinct may be to say: "Forget about this job, I'm sick of the problems there!" But don't be so quick! It's a tempting fantasy to believe that a "fresh start" somewhere else will be better. But, if you think back, you have probably had a number of jobs and problems (the same or different problems) developed at each one.

Even if you are fairly sure that you want to leave your current position, your "ADD-smart" move may be to stay for the time being. Why?

- You can practice building new success habits, and developing success traits on this job so that you will be in a better position to get and keep your next job.
- An improvement in performance and attitude will win you a much more positive recommendation when seeking another job.

What Really Needs to Change?

Your ADD Job Analysis is your blueprint for answering this question. Try to divide changes into two groups: internal and external.

External changes could include:

① Change of supervisor

② Using assistive technologies (computers, software, e-mail, electronic beepers, recorders, daily agendas, etc.)

③ More structure

④ More autonomy

⑤ Less distracting work environment

⑥ Change of coworkers

⑦ More interesting, challenging assignments

⑧ Less stressful work environment (define)

Think of more on your own. This list is just a start. Chapter 11 on accommodations and on assistive technology, may be helpful to you in devising this list.

Internal changes are those you make inside yourself. You need to ask: What kinds of changes do I need to make within myself?
Internal changes might include:

① Interacting differently with your supervisor.

② Developing ways to compensate for ADD problems.

③ Working on positive attitudes and habits. Look at Chapter 8 on "ADD Success Strategies"

④ Improving organizational and time management skills.

Some of these changes can be accomplished on your own, but you may find it helpful to work with an ADD job coach or specialist.

Putting It All Together

After you have gone through all these steps with your ADD career counselor, including a careful analysis of how ADD affects your functioning on your current job, considering possible learning disabilities, looking at your personality type, the best accommodations and coping strategies, and making a careful analysis of prior jobs, your counselor should be ready to write a highly detailed and specific report, carefully outlining what assistance your may need from a tutor or job coach, what coping strategies you should develop, and what reasonable accommodations you should need from your employer.

Your ADD career counselor should write an all-inclusive report for you, as well as a letter to your employer outlining the types of accommodations that are reasonable to help you achieve optimum performance at work. *Read Chapter 14 carefully before you decide whether to disclose your ADD to your employer in order to request accommodations.*

An ADD Career Assessment

In contrast to those who limit their focus to their current job, you may be asking a much broader question: "What would be the 'ideal' job for me?" or "Should I change careers?" When your focus is on finding the "right" job rather than adjusting better to your current job, you will need a broader ADD career assessment.

What Needs to Be Considered in a Career Assessment?

All of you, not just your ADD, needs to be considered in an ADD career assessment. An assessment that only focuses on ADD symptoms won't be very useful if you are poorly matched with your career. Although good career match is important for everyone, it is *essential* for adults with ADD. Why? It is almost *impossible* for an adult with ADD to succeed in a career that doesn't interest him or her! A good match should take advantage of your strengths, minimize your areas of weakness, and be interesting enough to "grab" your attention.

If you desire a full career evaluation, the process you go through should include all of the assessment techniques discussed previously, plus an evaluation of interests and abilities.

1. Interests

There are a number of "interest tests" that you can take. They are often offered at university counseling centers and by career counselors. Many psychologists also have been trained in interpreting interest testing. Three of the most common interest tests are the Self-Directed Search, the Strong Vocational Interest Blank, and the Vocational Preference Inventory. In general, these tests compare your stated interests with the interests of people who have been successful in various career fields. They provide you with a list of careers which most closely match your stated interests.

In his classic book, *What Color Is Your Parachute?* Richard Bolles describes less formal ways of analyzing interest patterns. One of these exercises is to imagine a party where there are six "types" of people (based on the interest tests mentioned above). He then asks you to imagine yourself at this party and to decide which groups of people you would feel most drawn to, in order from "most" to "least." The initials used to identify the first three groups on your preference list make up your "Holland code" or career type. Your choices of "groups" at this imaginary party are:

"Realistic" types—People who are mechanically or athletically oriented. They prefer to work with tools, plants, machines, and often prefer to be outdoors.

"Investigative" types—People who like to analyze, learn, investigate, and problem-solve. Many of these "investigators" are scientists.

"Artistic" types—People who are intuitive, creative, imaginative, and unstructured.

"Social" types—People who enjoy working with people and are good with words. They are often teachers, counselors, ministers, or other types of helpers.

"**Enterprising**" types—These people like to influence, persuade, manage, or lead others in business enterprises.

"**Conventional**" types—People who like to work with data, facts, details, and are comfortable carrying out instructions.

By imagining what group you would feel most drawn to and most comfortable with at this imaginary party, you are indirectly assessing your own cluster of interests and tendencies.

There is no "right" way to assess interests. Taking a test is not necessarily more accurate than the "imaginary party" exercise described by Bolles. Take a look at checklists in a number of books on choosing careers. No matter how you decide to assess your interests, do it in an active fashion, and take the idea of analyzing your interests seriously. A high degree of career interest is more important for an adult with ADD than for anyone else. Why? A high interest level is one of the most powerful antidotes to ADD!

2. Abilities

When you are concerned about ADD it is easy to dwell too much on the things you don't do well and forget to focus on your skills and abilities.

Do a personal skills assessment. Make a list of things that you do well (and *like* to do). Don't leave anything out just because it doesn't seem applicable to a career. Make as complete a list as you can. It may be useful to talk to a close friend or family member who may remind you of things you are overlooking. Your list might include things like:

Enjoy talking with people

Good at making people laugh

Good with my hands

Good cook

Read well

Good at writing

Good at taking care of young children

Good driver

Good at crossword puzzles

Good at playing Trivial Pursuit

Good athlete

In addition to this self-assessment, it may be very useful to take one of a number of ability tests that are available. One of the best known is offered by the Johnson-O'Connor Research Foundation. Another ability test is the Highlands Ability Battery. Both of these test batteries measure your ability across a wide range of activities. Their reports cluster your abilities and match these clusters with careers that call for such talents.

3. Personal Circumstances

Even after you have gathered all the information regarding interests and abilities, you still have important choices to make. For example, an assessment which concludes that you are ideally suited to become an architect isn't helpful if the time and resources aren't available to you to train for this career! A good assessment helps you choose the best fit for you within realistic options, considering personal factors such as:

Age.

Health.

Financial resources.

Time availability—considering other commitments, such as family commitments.

Feasibility/desirability of additional education or training.

The ideal career match must be realistic, taking into account all of your personal circumstances.

Summary

To summarize, an ADD Career Assessment should help you to consider carefully all of the following issues:

❶ How you are specifically affected at work by ADD.

❷ Whether your work performance is impacted by learning disabilities.

❸ What ADD coping strategies would be best for you.

❹ What on-the-job accommodations would be appropriate.

❺ What your work history reveals about jobs that are ADD-friendly for you.

❻ Your personality type and how it impacts a career choice.

❼ Which career choices are compatible with your interests.

❽ What is your unique mosaic of abilities and weaknesses.

❾ The impact of your personal circumstances upon career options.

The summary of your ADD Career Assessment should list which career options are a good match for you, that is, those which call primarily upon your greatest strengths while minimizing performance demands in your areas of weakness.

The process of making a good career choice or career change is complex. Taking time to work with your ADD career counselor following the assessment phase will be time well spent. Resist a typical ADD tendency to leap to a decision, and carefully consider, with your counselor, all of the factors listed above. Finding the ideal career match is well worth the work involved. A good career match (and job match within that career) can make all the difference in reaching a successful and satisfying work life.

A Good Career Match versus a Good Job Match.

There's a big difference between a **job** and a **career**. Often people confuse the two. You could be in the "right career", but in the "wrong job." What's the difference? A "career" is a very broad collection of "jobs," which all relate to the same general field. For example, you might choose a career in the computer field. There are many different jobs within this career field, however. You could be a programmer, a technician, a sales person, an administrator, a software developer, or a teacher or trainer. The same is true for almost every "career field"—there are a broad range of jobs within that field. Your task, as an adult with ADD, is to find a career field that interests you, and then to find a particular type of job within that field that is a good match for your strengths and interests.

If you are still in school and are in the process of choosing a career path, you need to think about both a *career* and about finding a particular *job* within that career. If you are already out in the working world your first question will probably be: "How can I function better in my current job?" Later, if you and your ADD career counselor conclude that you are very poorly matched with your current job/career you may want to consider a job change, or even a career change.

If You Have Concluded That Your Current Job is Impossible . . .

Don't give in to the impulse to start "completely fresh" until you have given some thought to less drastic changes. Consider a transfer within your organization. Consider a similar job in another organization. Changing jobs and changing careers can be extremely costly and time consuming.

The range of changes listed here are from least costly to most costly in terms of time, effort, and money. The more costly the type of job change you choose, however, the more investigation and research you should do before making final commitments. It is amazing, considering how costly it is to earn an undergraduate or graduate degree today, how casually many people make such a choice.

Range of Changes

1 Make changes in your current job.

2 Transfer to a different job in your same organization.

3 Find a related job in a more ADD-friendly organization.

4 Shift to unrelated work that doesn't require more training.

5 Change to a job that requires short-term, specialized training.

6 Choose a career path that requires you to earn an undergraduate or graduate degree.

There are a number of books that may be helpful to you in considering your options. Kate Kelly and Peggy Ramundo, both adults with ADD, discuss a variety of work options in their book *You Mean I'm Not Lazy, Stupid or Crazy?!*[1] Thom Hartmann discusses the appeal of entrepreneurial enterprises for adults with ADD in his book *Focus Your Energy*[2] Other books that do not focus specifically on ADD issues, but that explore career lifestyle alternatives are *Making a Living Without a Job,*[3] *Do What You Love, The Money Will Follow,*[4] *The Joy of Working From Home,*[5] and the career search classic, already mentioned, *What Color Is Your Parachute?*.[6]

Think About Job "Evolution" Instead of an Abrupt Job Change.

While some people make abrupt, distinct job changes—say from salesman to educator—for many other people their career is a process of evolution.

One young man with ADD began his adult life as a rock musician. He actually achieved some measure of success for a few years, but tired of the hectic, stressful life. He quit performing and began earning a living recording other groups and renting practice and recording space.

As his siblings began having children he became very involved with his nephews and nieces and began writing humorous children's songs for them. They were such a hit in the family that he began performing in local public schools. He developed a second performing career which did not entail the rugged performance schedule of a rock musician.

In his second performance career he met a young teacher with whom he fell in love and married. She became the director of a child care center. His open schedule allowed him much free time. He began playing at the child care center, found he loved the work with children, and eventually decided to go back to school to study early childhood education. The songs he had written for children were of great interest to the school of education he attented, and became the subject of his senior project. Ten years after dropping out of college to pursue his rock career, his career has evolved, very naturally, and in stages, to a radically different, but even more satisfying career.

Don't Let Yourself Become Paralyzed by Choice!

Remember, you're not making a choice for *forever*, you're making a choice for right now. Think in terms of making *better* choices rather than making the *perfect* choice. Your needs and priorities will change over the course of your life. At certain times, when you have young children, for example, priorities such as a short commute may be high on your list. Later you may feel the freedom to accept a job which entails travel. At certain times your priorities may lead you to select a part-time position, at other times you may need to maximize your income because you have children close to college age.

What is described in this chapter is meant to be an ongoing *process* through which you learn and grow, not a single *choice* that you make, and then must forever live with the consequences. So go ahead, take the plunge, and best of luck in creating or finding a good job match for you!

What if People Tell Me I'm Unrealistic in What I Want?

Some people settle for so little in their work life. Jobs are certainly work and not play, but looking for a place where we can truly be comfortable, and truly apply our gifts is a great pleasure and satisfaction in life. Finding a job that is interesting is even more essential when you have ADD. You can't expect perfection, but neither should you be talked out of looking for real job satisfaction.

Don't let people who don't understand ADD convince you that you're wrong in your reactions. ADD is a very "reactive" disorder. Some workplace factors, which can be fairly easily accommodated or overlooked by others, may be truly intolerable to someone with ADD. Your reactions may be entirely valid for you, even though they greatly differ from the reactions of others. Many people with ADD are highly sensitive to such distractions as noise level, disorder, fluorescent lighting, emotional discord, distractions, and stress. It is well worth your while, and not a self-indulgence, to look for a work environment that is your brand of "ADD-friendly." It is one thing to expect the world to accommodate your every whim. It is another to take responsibility for yourself and your life and to actively seek a work environment in which you can flourish.

If people tell you that hardly any of us find the "perfect job" they're right. But having a thorough understanding of your needs, preferences, desires, strengths, and foibles can help you enormously, both in your current job, and in any job you seek. Knowing your needs doesn't mean you'll find a job that meets all of them, but you're much less likely to find a good job match if you don't even understand what your needs are!

Don't Lose Track of What You Really Love to Do!

Don't lose sight of the fact, however, that *doing what you love*, is probably the best recipe for success of all. I don't mean this in some idealistic, impractical sense. I just mean to emphasize the enormous importance of *motivation* for adults with ADD in overcoming their other difficulties and hurdles. There is no greater motivation than doing what you really *want* to do!

An ADD Workplace Assessment or Career Assessment should begin an ongoing process through which you learn and grow. What is best for you will almost certainly change as you go through your work life. Don't let yourself be frightened or paralyzed by choices or changes. Each change is rarely permanent, but rather just the next step in an evolving career. So—best of luck in finding a good workplace or career assessment that can start you down the path to job satisfaction!

IN THIS CHAPTER

In this chapter, coping techniques are suggested for dealing with the problem areas covered by the ADD Workplace Questionnaire in the Appendix. It may be useful to complete this questionnaire before reading Chapters 3, 4 and 5.

3

Taking Charge of Your ADD:
Job Performance

T his chapter focuses primarily on ways to perform your work more efficiently. Keep in mind that ADD is not manifested identically in all people. Some of the patterns described may apply to you while others may not. Focus on those sections that correspond to your particular concerns.

Inattention/Distractibility

P roblems with distractibility can be either external (distractions in the environment) or internal (distractions due to internal thoughts, reactions, or daydreams).

External Distractions

Distractibility is a difficult issue for many ADD adults. The mental energy drained from an ADD adult in a distracting environment with frequent interruptions can significantly detract from his or her ability to be efficient and productive. Here are some suggestions for managing environmental distractions:

- Shift your work hours in order to increase distraction-free time at the office.

- Work from home part of the time.

- Use headphones to help screen distracting sounds.

- Use a fan or white-noise machine to muffle sounds.

- Request a private office, if available.

- Use conference rooms, or unused private offices when available.

- Shift your work space to a less trafficked area.

- Request sound-absorbing portable office partitions.

- Request an office mate whose work habits are less distracting.

- Face your desk away from the office door or the line of traffic.

- Use foam earplugs.

Internal Distractions

Many ADD adults struggle as much from internal as from external distractions:

- **"Ahha!" Distractions**   Creative ideas that take you off-task can be managed by writing your ideas down before you return to your current task. By managing your "ahha's," they can become a real asset rather than a distraction from current work.

- **"Oh no!" Distractions**   The sudden intrusive memory of a forgotten task. Your solution can be found in learning to effectively use a day-planning system to record tasks, phone calls, meetings, and so on, so that you are less likely to forget.

- **"Ho hum" Distractions**   Work avoidant daydreams. Your solution will come in finding ways to make your work more interesting or in seeking more interesting work elsewhere. Chronic daydreamers are often stuck in a poor job match.

Hyperfocusing

Hyperfocusing can lead to tremendous productivity, but it can also derail your daily schedule. Some adults with ADD report that they become so oblivious when working that they miss meetings and lunch appointments and otherwise lose all track of time. Less engaging aspects of your job tend to go entirely ignored, as you hyperfocus on what fascinates you. Here are some coping techniques:

- Look for a compatible work environment in which total immersion and lack of social interaction is acceptable.

- Learn to cue yourself. This might mean setting an alarm or perhaps asking a coworker to tap on your shoulder or your door as he or she leaves for a meeting or lunch.

- Plan your periods of hyperfocusing so that they don't interfere with scheduled commitments.

- Get the boring stuff out of the way, then hyperfocus to your heart's content.

Impulsivity

Extreme impulsivity can be very destructive. Highly impulsive individuals make even major life decisions without much thought of consequences. They may repeatedly leave jobs on impulse, never staying long enough to find solutions or compromises; they commit to projects or tasks without considering whether they have the time or resources. Impulsivity can lead to great inefficiency. Jumping into a project without forethought or planning leads to blunders, ineffectiveness, and disorganization. Here are some some coping techniques to manage impulsivity:

- Impulsive job-hopping. Learn to better understand your needs. Analyze whether a job is suitable for you *before* accepting it. If you need work immediately consider temping while you work to better understand your needs and talents. If you are more thoughtful in accepting your next job, you will be less likely to quit impulsively.

- Making impulsive commitments. Rather than giving an automatic "yes," learn a catchphrase such as "I'd like to, but let me take a look at my calendar." This phrase can act as a set of brakes for you. With a little time for reflection, you'll be able to make sounder decisions.

- Jumping in without a plan. This lack of planning can be a very inefficient way of doing things and is discussed more fully under the section, "Problems with Organization" later in this chapter.

- General impulsivity. In general, the rule is to slow down and consider. If you have already acted impulsively—by making a misguided commitment or decision, go back and "undo" it quickly. Changing your impulsive commitment or decision at the outset is much less damaging, before others have already committed time and energy to your impulsive plan.

Hyperactivity

Unfortunately, for some people with ADD, the majority of jobs today are sedentary. Hyperactive ADD adults are poorly suited to such environments. Their tapping, walking, and wandering can easily be interpreted negatively as boredom, disinterest, or low motivation. Additionally, when they do things at a quick pace, they sometimes frustrate or fluster coworkers who work at a more measured pace. Here are some techniques for coping with hyperactivity:

- "Fidget" intentionally by taking notes during meetings (this not only will give you an activity but also will enhance your concentration).

- Do things that require movement—picking up the mail, going to the copy machine, getting a cup of coffee—when you need a break from sedentary activity.

- Bring your lunch and exercise during your lunch break.

- If you have a private office, take brief exercise breaks every hour or two.

- Build more movement and activity into your life; for example, park further away from the office and walk to work from there.

- Engage in athletic activities after work.

- People with ADD who are extremely restless should look for types of work that routinely allow movement; work in sales, construction, repair, servicing, law enforcement, and fire protection may be a good fit.

- Work two part-time jobs rather than one full-time job, to increase movement and variety.

Need for Stimulation (Intolerance of Routine)

Many jobs entail repetitive, uninteresting work. People who have a low tolerance for this may be perceived as "spoiled" or poorly motivated. Many adults with ADD grow bored by the daily management and follow-through tasks which follow the creative, exciting start-up phase of projects. Here are some suggestions:

- If you have the opportunity, team up with a coworker whose strengths are in your areas of weakness (look for a partner who is good at details and day-to-day management).

- If you do not have this luxury, look for assistance or training to improve your skills in organization.

- If possible, choose work that allows a high degree of change and variety.

- Look for work that calls for a minimum of record keeping and paperwork.

- If you work for yourself, hire someone to manage the details and keep the records.

Memory Difficulties

O ften many ADD adults exhibit poor short-term memory; they absentmindedly misplace items, lock their keys in their car, or forget to carry through on verbal requests from others. Frequent forgetting at work can be misperceived as irresponsibility or poor motivation. The following list shows practical approaches that some adults with ADD have found helpful.

3 JOB PERFORMANCE

Tips for Combatting Poor Short-Term Memory

1 Carry a day planner with you at *all* times.

2 Avoid situations where you receive information without the chance to write it down.

3 Don't write notes on scraps of paper—only in your day planner.

4 Always take notes during meetings.

5 Ask coworkers to e-mail or fax rather than to call.

6 Avoid interruptions whenever possible. Close your door, send calls to voice mail.

7 Use a tape recorder.

8 Develop a beeper or reminder system on your watch or computer to cue you regarding scheduled tasks or events.

9 Use visual prompts—post-it notes. Place reminder objects where you'll see them. By the front door. In the front seat of your car.

10 Visualize to pre-rehearse a sequence of things you need to do.

11 Develop routines. They place less demand on memory.

Time Management

Running Late

"Running late" is an almost classic ADD symptom. There are several coping techniques:

- Plan to arrive early to allow for unforeseen events. If none occur, you will arrive early, allowing time to plan, focus, take notes, or reread the memo, which well help you to organize and improve your work performance.

- Don't give in to the "just-one-more-thing" impulse. If you think of one more thing to do as you prepare to leave, write down your idea in your day timer and act on it later.

- Be on the lookout for impulses that occur on the way to do something else. One man with ADD found that even after he had mastered leaving for work early, he still on occasion arrived at the office late because he gave in to impulses on the way.

- Build in "getting ready" time. For some adults with ADD, the "it's time to go" cue often becomes their cue to get ready. Only then do they ask themselves such questions as "What do I need to take with me?" and "What is the phone number in case I get lost?" These questions are important, but they should be asked—and answered—before it's time to walk out the door.

Overcommitment

Another classic ADD time management problem is overcommitment, that is, deciding to do things that you really don't have time to do and then attempting to squeeze them in, anyway. Whether this kind of over-commitment occurs on a large scale at work or on a small scale with friends or family, it can wreak havoc with conducting life in some kind of orderly fashion. Here are a couple of techniques to help you cope with overcommitment:

▤ Make it a habit to say, "Let me check my other commitments," before accepting a new one.

▤ Try to catch yourself before giving in to an impulse to squeeze something into your busy schedule. Finish the already scheduled things first. Then, if you have time, you can add other things to your list.

▤ If you add a commitment, then you must subtract a previous one. Your time is not infinitely expandable.

Procrastination

Procrastination is a major time management problem for many people with ADD, especially for tasks that are difficult or uninteresting.

Here are some coping techniques for managing a tendency to procrastinate:

▤ Look for jobs in which there is a minimum of tedious paperwork—the number one procrastination item.

▤ Look for jobs in which there are few long-term projects requiring a large report at the end, another item that typically poses major problems for ADD procrastinators.

▤ Commit yourself to a deadline and declare it to colleagues or to your supervisor. Making a promise to others often helps people overcome their own resistance.

Paperwork Problems at Work

Paperwork poses typical problems for adults with ADD. These can range from relatively minor ones (e.g., turning in your expense record or time sheet late) to major ones, such as losing important material or not completing paperwork critical to the functioning of your organization.

Why do these problems happen? A number of ADD traits come together to create the paperwork pile: impatience with detail; a tendency to put off doing boring, unessential things; a tendency to toss papers on your desk to deal with later rather than take care of them as soon as they arrive.

To cope with this problem, you can try the following:

▨ Look for work that has a minimum of paperwork.

▨ Look for ways to streamline your job to reduce paperwork.

▨ Find ways to reward yourself for completing unavoidable paperwork.

▨ Develop a more streamlined filing system to make your filing chores easier and less tedious.

▨ Do tedious tasks regularly, in small bits—do not let the filing or correspondence pile up and become overwhelming.

Problems with Organization

Many ADD adults have a tendency to jump into tasks and figure them out as they go. This approach can work for some relatively simple tasks and can be tolerated in complicated tasks in which the ADD adult is working solo. The impromptu approach is more likely to fail, however, when the project is complex or must be coordinated with the work of others. Here are some tips to consider if you have problems with organization:

▨ Start at the end and work backwards. Mark on a calendar when your project is due and then work backward, indicating on the calendar the various dates by which earlier stages must be completed. This approach often results in a more realistic time line.

▨ Make it visual. For many adults with ADD, "out of sight is out of mind." Make a large chart of time lines for all of your projects, and place it on the wall of your cubicle or office so that you can readily check what needs to be done when.

- Divide projects into bite-sized tasks. Reward yourself for the completion of each task.
- Prioritize and plan with a coworker or supervisor.

Difficulty with Long-Term Follow-Through

Some behavior patterns that may appear to be procrastination are actually a product of distractibility and poor organization. An ADD adult may have a host of projects that have been left undone because his flow of ideas have led him further and further away from his original task. He may be simply caught up in the project of the moment and may have little or none of the negative, avoidant pattern present in procrastination. Such ADD adults are often enthusiastic, energetic initiators who, being drawn from one interesting idea or impulse to the next, are simply ineffective in task completion. If this description fits you, consider these tips:

- Use a day planning system religiously.
- Take a course in time management and organization.
- Work with a partner or group that can help keep you on task.
- Establish a pattern of daily or weekly reporting to your supervisor to help keep you focused.

Difficulty Coordinating Simultaneous Tasks

Many bright, capable ADD adults encounter severe performance problems in the workplace when they are promoted to managerial positions in which they are expected to coordinate multiple projects and people. Jobs that require ADD adults to oversee many people in several different projects may over-tax their organizational capacity. They may encounter enormous difficulty monitoring both their own progress and the progress of the rest of the team involved in a complex, long-term project.

ADD adults may frequently have the feeling that they have been frantically busy all day but have accomplished little. In fact, their disorganization and forgetfulness may have created crises to which they then had to respond, further distracting them from attending to other aspects of their complex job. If you have difficulty coordinating several tasks at once, consider the following suggestions:

- Be realistic in assessing your managerial abilities. No matter how tempting a managerial position may seem initially, it may in the end bring more frustration than satisfaction.

- Try shifting the responsibility to your supervisees to "check in" with you rather than wait for you to "check up" on them.

- Divide your day: Begin with supervisory tasks and then move to your own work. If you begin your own work first, you may find that you have hyperfocused, overlooking your supervisory responsibilities.

- Carefully protect yourself from constant interruptions by those whom you supervise. Set aside times when you are available.

Conclusion

In this chapter I have tried to deal in a limited space with a wide range of job performance difficulties often experienced by individuals with ADD. The suggestions here are by no means exhaustive. Memory, time management, procrastination, planning, and organizational skills are all complex issues. Entire books have been devoted to each of them. The suggestions here are meant as a starting point for you. In order to succeed in really changing some of these troubling work patterns, you will need to devote extended time; moreover, you are likely to need the assistance of a tutor, counselor, or coach. Here are a few general suggestions for you:

- Don't try to tackle everything at once. Successes tend to build, one on top of the other. For example, better time management on your part will enhance your later efforts toward better organization and planning.

- Build habits. Pick a crucial area, identify some practical approaches, and then keep at it until you have developed a new habit.

- Use others to keep you focused. A coach or counselor may be useful to help you figure out where things are going wrong and to suggest a different approach.

- Be realistic. Some people with ADD, determined to master their difficulties, create their own downfall by sticking with a job for which they are poorly suited. Your efforts will be much better spent if you choose a job wisely, one that calls upon your strengths, and then work on habit building in an ADD-friendly environment.

Many adults with ADD find that they are most effective in beginning to implement some of these approaches when they work regularly with a therapist and/or an ADD coach, who helps them to prioritize, keep focused, and problem-solve when things go wrong.

Remember, don't try to do too many things at once, and don't try to do it all alone. Habits take time to build! If you are patient with yourself, you may be very pleased to recognize how much better organized and efficient you are a year or so from now.

IN THIS CHAPTER

This chapter focuses on the effects of ADD on work productivity from an interpersonal perspective. Social and communication patterns sometimes found in adults with ADD are discussed and suggestions are offered for ways to improve your social interactions at work.

Taking Charge of Your ADD: Social Skills

In the preceding chapter we considered a range of ADD traits (and patterns often found associated with ADD) in terms of their direct effect on job performance. An essential part of performing your job, however, depends on your ability to work well with others. Let's go back, then, and reconsider these same ADD traits from an interpersonal point of view.

Why All This Emphasis on Social Skills?

In their book *When Smart People Fail*, Carole Hyatt and Linda Gottlieb describe their investigation of career failures among a group of smart, talented people in a broad range of professions.[1] They concluded that the most critical factor, by far, in career failure is related to interpersonal problems. No matter how talented and capable you may be, you cannot afford to ignore the importance of learning how to cooperate with others, to read social cues, to work as a team member, to remain aware of how your attitudes and habits affect those you work with.

Social skills can be even more critical for adults with ADD. By paying attention to your effect on others, by cooperating with them, and by showing consideration and tolerance of differences, you can build up goodwill, like credit in the bank, that you can later draw on if your ADD inadvertently causes problems for others. If your coworkers know you, feel close to you, like you, and trust you, then you have a lot more leeway to make mistakes—and opportunity to learn from those mistakes. By making sure that your positives outweigh the negatives, some of your mistakes will be either tolerated or overlooked.

**Building credits
through positive
work relations
prevents ADD slip-ups
from overdrawing
your "goodwill account"
at work.**

Tuning In to Your Effect on Others in the Workplace

The majority of the interpersonal difficulties created by adults with ADD are completely unintentional and are often created even without awareness.[2] In fact, awareness of behavior patterns that may cause interpersonal difficulties is the first and most crucial step toward reducing those patterns. Let's look at some of the most common ways someone with ADD might unintentionally step on others' toes at work.

After reading this chapter, if you recognize some of these patterns in yourself, it may be useful for you to work with a counselor on making changes. Additionally, if you have a trusted coworker who can give you a friendly hint when you are overstepping boundaries in the workplace, you can make a correction more quickly. A quick, sincere apology followed by genuine efforts to change a problem behavior will go a long way toward smoothing ruffled feathers.

Good Citizenship at Work

In any discussion of social skills in the workplace, a good place to start is with the basics—the nuts and bolts of good manners and the basic ingredients of good citizenship in the organization. The workplace is a community of individuals engaged in interconnected, cooperative efforts who must spend the majority of their waking hours together. Learning to pay attention to the basics of good citizenship in that community is essential to improving your functioning as an adult with ADD.

Good citizenship at work may at times be more challenging for adults with ADD. Why? Because good citizenship involves attention to complex group interactions. It involves continuously monitoring your effect on others while you simultaneously go about your work. For adults with ADD this dual focus is often difficult to maintain. They may become so intent on the point they are making in a verbal discussion that they are unaware that they have become argumentative rather than persuasive. Likewise, they may become so wrapped up in their work that they forget, for example, that they have promised to phone a colleague. Furthermore, they may be completely unaware that their tapping, fidgeting, or chair tipping is annoying to those around them.

ADD Patterns and Interpersonal Friction in the Workplace

Let's take a look at some of the ADD patterns that may cause problems in the interpersonal arena at work.

Punctuality

Is "Always late, but worth the wait" your motto? Well, don't bank on it, or you'll run your "good will account" into the debit column. No

matter how hard you work or how brilliant your contribution, the impressions you make through lateness tend to endure. Chronic lateness suggests lack of discipline, lack of organization, and lack of professionalism. Routinely arriving late for meetings gives the impression that you consider your time more valuable than that of your coworkers. Some time management suggestions are shown on page 46.

**Make your
new motto—
"On time
all the time."**

Procrastination

Putting *things* off puts *people* off![3] While many ADD adults are quite aware of their tendency to procrastinate and the problems it causes *them*, they may be less aware of the negative impact their procrastination has on others. These patterns almost always have a negative impact on coworkers. Unless your projects are entirely independent (which is rarely the case), your procrastination is likely to create frustration and resentment among the other members of your team. Often they cannot complete some portion of their own work until they have received yours.

One man caused such frustration among his fellow researchers by completing his work consistently late over the course of years that several members of his team went to great lengths to terminate their long-term relationship with him.

- Create a series of intermediate deadlines.
- Meet regularly with team members and set short-term goals; weekly goals, and even daily ones, can be very helpful in avoiding procrastination on large long-term projects.

4 SOCIAL SKILLS

Tips for Time Management

☐ Take time management step-by-step. Good time management requires building a whole set of habits and can't be done overnight.

☐ Let your supervisor and coworkers know that you take your time problems seriously and are working hard to change your habits.

☐ A good place to start is by arriving at work on time. Running late in the morning may be related to a number of things:

    *Getting to bed too late the night before (you may have sleep problems that need treatment)

    *Habitual "escapist" activities at night that make you tired the next day (computer games, television, detective books, and so on)

    *Not allowing enough time in the morning

    *Allowing distractions to get in the way in the morning

    *Never allowing extra time for traffic jams, or other unforeseen events

☐ Try to arrive early for all events. Many people with ADD hate to wait and therefore avoid being early. As a result, they are often late. Bring something to read or work on so that if you succeed in arriving early, you won't feel impatient.

☐ Try to pinpoint patterns that lead to chronic lateness, for example:

    *Answering the phone when you're on your way out the door

    *Impulsively trying to do one more thing before you leave

    *Getting involved in some activity—reading the paper, watching the news, engaging in conversation—and then losing track of the time

■ Identify activities that are most likely to produce procrastination (these are often tasks that involve paperwork, such as writing summaries, reports, articles, or budgets) and try to organize the project so that you have reduced responsibility for such tasks.

■ Team up with someone who is less likely to procrastinate.

■ Volunteer for activities that are immediate and that therefore cannot be put off.

■ Don't expect your procrastination to be tolerated. Apologize when it occurs and make genuine efforts to make amends.

Remember:

**Putting *things* off
Puts *people* off.**[3]

When You Are the Newcomer

When you begin a new job, you have entered foreign territory. Until you have been on the job long enough to be an insider, it is important to recognize your newcomer status. This means getting the lay of the land, understanding the politics of your new office environment, before venturing to express your own opinions. This prolonged period of reticence can be difficult for some adults with ADD. By impulsively expressing their opinions or asking indiscreet questions they may unwittingly offend their coworkers, thereby making their acceptance in the new work environment more difficult. Here are some tips for newcomers:

■ If you have ideas for changes or innovations, write them down. This will help you restrain yourself, and they may prove valuable later.

- Look for someone who seems friendly and approachable. He or she may be able to introduce you to the interpersonal landscape of your new job.

- Engage in self-talk. Remind yourself repeatedly that you need to "stop, look, and listen" rather than barge in too soon.

- Don't jump in with both feet. They may not like the splash you make!

Before you jump in . . .
Count to 10.

Space and Time Invasion

Many ADD adults may unintentionally create in others a feeling of being invaded. Without awareness or intention, adults with ADD are prone to interrupt conversations, borrow items (owing to their disorganization) and forget to return them, and spread their belongings around in a way that interferes with others. These tendencies are among the behaviors that you should be hypervigilant about, especially when you enter a new work environment. Consider the following solutions:

- Look for ways to confine your work and belongings to a circumscribed area.

- Make it a top priority to obtain needed items for yourself rather than continue to borrow from others.

- Always ask first—don't assume it's OK to use or borrow something.

- Always ask, "Have you got a minute?" Then keep it to a *minute*!

■ Look *closely* for cues that your coworker is busy and wants to terminate the discussion.

Need for Stimulation (Intolerance of Routine)

Due to a strong need for stimulation, some adults with ADD can stir up extra work and extra trouble for coworkers. You may cause resentment as you leave the "dirty work" to others while you buzz off to create something new and interesting. To avoid such resentment:

■ Don't just assume that someone else will pick up the pieces.

■ Look for jobs in which your assigned work is stimulating so that you are not continually looking for other tasks.

■ Take on your fair share of the work that no one really cares to do!

■ Be aware that others are not comfortable with your fast pace and need for stimulation.

■ Be careful not to make more work for others as you seek new projects for yourself.

Paperwork

The extent to which your difficulty in handling paperwork affects others depends on how important completion of paperwork is to your job function. Nevertheless, your paperwork problems are bound to have a negative impact to some extent in any job. No matter how well you do other aspects of your job, if you misfile, don't file, can't find important documents, don't turn in time sheets routinely, and miss details, you will likely be seen as careless and as someone who can't really be depended on. Here are some coping techniques:

■ Keep your filing system as simple as possible so that you will be more likely to file. (One man with ADD developed a filing system that consisted of a dozen boxes, clearly labeled and kept on shelves. Although it was not an elegant system, he found that he could at least get himself to toss papers in the appropriate box whereas with a more traditional filing system he tended to accumulate unfiled stacks of paper randomly situated throughout his office.)

■ Filing systems that are easily accessible seem to work best. (Some ADD adults work well with files in open carts, which can be seen and easily accessed.)

■ Color-coded filing systems often work better for adults with ADD. (Color code by broad category; for example, have one color for files you need to access frequently.)

■ Whenever possible, avoid jobs that entail a great deal of filing and paperwork.

■ If you file early in the day, the chore is more likely to get done.

 **Minimize paperwork
to maximize success.**

Organization

An ADD adult's problems with organization have the same sorts of impact on coworkers as his or her problems with time management and paperwork. Your own disorganization spills over and affects the work of others. By working reactively rather than proactively, you are consciously or unconsciously depending on others to cue you as to what to do next.

■ The single most important thing you can do to improve your organization is to buy a day planner, take a training course on its use, and actively work toward the habit of using it to plan your day, week, and month.

▓ Adopt a "do it now or write it down" rule.

▓ Look for ways to simplify your job—disorganization increases with complexity.

▓ Ask for assistance from your supervisor in setting work priorities.

Learn to:
Plan
↓
Prioritize
↓
Proceed

Tuning Others Out

Some people with ADD become so task focused that they overlook the tremendous importance of keeping the social wheels oiled at the office. This doesn't mean that you have to join in the gossip at the water-cooler, but a friendly smile and a quick hello are essential to good working relationships.

If you unintentionally ignore others while hyperfocusing on your work, it will require an active effort on your part to change your pattern. Recognizing that social interaction in the workplace is essential is the first step (some people with ADD tend to live in a cocoon of preoccupation, with little awareness of the reactions of others).

You cannot operate effectively in an organization if you are in a social vacuum. Through interaction with others you develop networks, partnerships, and alliances and learn of important events and changes in the organization. Once you make a decision to change your social patterns, it will take conscious effort to develop new habits. Some approaches:

- Make a regular lunch date with coworkers.

- Arrive early at meetings in order to have an opportunity to talk.

- Make a conscious effort to greet people in the morning and to say good-bye before departing in the evening.

**Oiling social wheels
will keep
your project
running smoothly.**

Distracting Others from Their Work

For others with ADD the problem is not ignoring coworkers but talking to them too much. Some people with ADD, particularly those who are extroverts, have a strong need to talk about ideas that have occurred to them. They may become so engrossed in expressing themselves that they ignore the nonverbal social cues that their listener has work to do and would like to terminate the discussion. If you have this problem, here are some coping techniques:

- If you need to talk, go to a place where social interaction is expected (e.g., the lounge or coffee shop).

- Avoid monopolozing the time of support staff and recognize that many have desks in open areas because much of their work requires that they be available to others. Catch yourself if you have a tendency, owing to your ADD talkativeness, to stretch a friendly greeting into a 20-minute monologue.

- Write down your ideas.

- Make regular lunch dates where longer conversations are appropriate.

Look for work that entails a high degree of interpersonal interaction.

4 SOCIAL SKILLS

**Don't let
"Got a minute?"
turn into
twenty minutes.**

Memory Difficulties

Not remembering important details others have told you, not remembering to follow through on promises you have made, not remembering to return borrowed items—all of these are typical and unintentional behaviors. Yet they can lead to tremendous resentment on the part of your coworkers if they recur repeatedly. What can you do? Your memory will never become perfect, but there are a number of things you can do to ease the situation (for more suggestions, refer to the section on memory in Chapter 3).

 Ask for things in writing.

 Write things down yourself—in a consistent, well-organized fashion (e.g., by using a day planner).

 Apologize sincerely, and make amends through some small gesture if your memory lapse has negatively affected someone else.

 **Do it now,
or
write it down!**

Hyperactivity/Restlessness

Your hyperactivity and restlessness can lead to clear expressions of your impatience with others or of your intolerance of the slow process of group decision making. Some ADD adults may come across like a bulldozer, pushing people to "get to the point" and badgering them with questions like "What's taking so long?" and exclamations like "Let's go; I don't have all day!" If you recognize yourself in this description, here are some suggestions:

- Look for work that allows a high degree of independent functioning.
- Explain your restlessness with humor so that coworkers don't misinterpret it as disinterest.
- Volunteer for those aspects of group projects that require less interactive efforts.
- Look for a high energy work environment.
- Use self-talk and relaxation exercises to calm yourself in situations in which you are likely to become impatient (e.g., meetings).

Disappearing Acts

Restlessness and hyperactivity can also lead to "disappearing acts" at work. Do your boss and coworkers make jokes about never being able to find you? Being on-the-go may be a way you have learned to deal with your ADD, but if it comes at the expense of your coworkers, or if it gives the impression that you are goofing off, then you need to find a better coping device. Some suggestions:

- Establish that you really are working but need a change of scenery.
- Obtain permission to go home early or to work in a different part of the building.

- Always tell others where you can be found.
- Be sure to build exercise into each workday.

Social Faux Pas in Meetings

A good deal of the interpersonal interaction in an organization takes place in meetings. To many adults with ADD, meetings may seem pointless, inefficient, or boring. Some of the most common social faux pas committed by ADD adults in meetings are the following:

Becoming argumentative

Being too blunt or critical when disagreeing with a proposal

Repeated interrupting

Tuning out

Going off on verbal tangents

Try the following suggestions instead:

- Ask for feedback about your social behavior in meetings from a trusted friend or colleague as you try to become aware of and change your negative behaviors.
- Take notes at meetings to help slow you down, make you more aware of your thoughts before speaking, and help break your pattern of interrupting for fear you will lose the thought you wanted to express.
- Develop the habit of writing your ideas down before you express them. This will help focus your remarks, avoiding tangents; give you the added time to express yourself more diplomatically; and eliminate your need to blurt out your thought for fear you will forget it.

Other Problematic Communication Patterns

Launching into a Monologue

Some adults with ADD are prone to give long monologues. Once they launch into a topic, they become totally engrossed and are much less likely to attend to nonverbal cues that their listener has lost interest. Skilled conversation requires flexible shifting, eye contact, and on-going attention to the other person's responses. If you tend to mono-logue, try the following:

- Catch yourself before your monologue begins.
- Indicate to your trapped listener that you realize you've gone on far too long, and apologize with humor.
- Ask questions to allow your listener to change the subject.
- Look directly at the other person.
- Keep your focus on the other person's ideas and paraphrase what you have heard to show you've listened.

Distractibility

Many adults with ADD are highly distractible. While they are talking with someone at work, their attention may be uncontrollably drawn away by sights and sounds, giving an impression of disinterest. If this happens to you, try the following solutions:

- Explain that you are easily distracted.
- Suggest going to a less distracting place to continue the conversation.
- Be sure to give your coworkers the impression that you are interested in what they say.

▪ Suggest a specific time to continue the discussion if a coworker catches you when you are preoccupied.

Bluntness

Bluntness is saying the first thing that comes to mind without considering the possible consequences. Some adults with ADD, unfortunately, congratulate themselves on their "honesty" instead of recognizing the harm they may do to others—and the harm they are doing to themselves in the process. It is quite possible to be direct and honest without being destructively critical, angry, or belittling. Follow these steps:

▪ First, recognize that your bluntness is seldom seen as refreshing candor and is often harmful.

▪ Practice slowing down your responses in conversations. Give yourself time to stop and think.

▪ Do some advanced planning. If you need to broach a particularly sensitive topic with a coworker, think about what you'd like to say, write it down, and possibly even discuss your approach with someone else in order to find a constructive way to discuss a negative topic.

▪ If bluntness is the result of frustration or anger, remove yourself until you feel more calm.

Hypersensitivity to Criticism

Ironically, although some ADD adults can be blunt with others, they themselves are often hypersensitive to criticism or negative feedback. This hypersensitivity results both from a physiological predisposition to overreact emotionally and from a lifetime of criticism for ADD behaviors. Such hypersensitivity in the workplace can make relationships touchy and difficult.

If a colleague makes a mild complaint and your reaction is one of defensiveness, or anger, you have begun to create a relationship in which collaboration becomes less and less likely. It is the job of your direct supervisor to give you feedback, both positive and negative, if your reaction to negative feedback is emotional, defensive, or angry, your supervisor will begin to conclude that you are a difficult person to work with. To prevent these consequences, consider the following suggestions:

- If your reactions to criticism are intense, these are issues you may need to work on in therapy.

- Look for work with a supervisor who is calm and supportive.

- Look for ways to solve problems and ease the tensions before strong feelings develop.

- Lower your stress to lower your overreactions.

- Recognize and reduce your contact with people who lead you to overreact.

- Temper reactions in ADD adults can be triggered by work that requires them to function in an area of weakness for them, causing tension and frustration. Both stress and the overreaction to it are likely to increase when ADD adults feel they must keep their difficulty in functioning secret. (More about this in the next chapter on problems in cognitive functioning.)

- Avoid or minimize tasks which are difficult and frustrating; you're more prone to emotional reactions when functioning in an area of weakness.

**De-stress yourself,
so you don't
distress others**

Difficulty Accepting Guidance or Direction from Others

Some, but not all, adults with ADD prefer to operate independently and experience great difficulty in accepting the guidance or direction of others. ADD adults who choose to work alone run a risk, however, if they also have poor organizational skills and/or a strong tendency to procrastinate.

Finding the ideal balance between freedom and structure can prove difficult. Some ADD adults achieve this balance by collaborating with a well-selected business partner or office manager; not infrequently, the spouse fills this role.

There are some fields where there is no choice but to work in tandem with others and under the supervision of others. If you are in this position, here are some approaches you can take that may lessen your discomfort:

- The most important comfort factor lies in the match between yourself and your supervisor (read Chapter 10, The Ideal Boss).

- Depending on the strength of your reaction to feeling "micromanaged," the nature of your supervisor may be one of the most important factors to consider in looking for a good job match.

- Even in group projects there are certain tasks that require less interaction and coordination with others. Look for and request such tasks.

- Examine your own reactions to supervision. You may be able to alter defensive reactions to improve relations between you and your supervisor.

Conclusion

This chapter has discussed a range of potential interpersonal glitches that may be caused by certain types of ADD traits and reactions. The following points are intended as a general summary of ways to improve your interpersonal functioning in the workplace.

❶ Explain yourself.
Don't make excuses.
Recognize your effect on coworkers.
Explain that your patterns of reaction are sometimes out of your control.
Most importantly, explain that you are making efforts to change those patterns.

❷ Catch yourself. Just because you become aware of patterns doesn't mean they will automatically disappear! Don't become overly critical of yourself when you repeat problematic patterns. Just try to catch yourself and make a midcourse correction.

❸ Apologize. When you catch yourself doing something that may have bothered a coworker, acknowledge it and apologize. It is much easier for others to feel tolerant and supportive of ADD adults who are aware and concerned about their effect on their coworkers.

❹ Develop positive habits. Don't just focus on the negative. Deliberately look for positive interpersonal habits that can compensate, in some ways, for negative behaviors not completely under your control. Some adults with ADD learn these habits instinctively; they use humor, tell entertaining stories, extend friendly greetings, and take the time to pay attention to, and do small personal favors for others. If you are genuinely warm and friendly but still have trouble being on time for meetings or turning in your expense report, your ADD lapses will be balanced in the eyes of others by your efforts to consider them and their feelings.

❺ Look for work that is more independent in nature. There is tremendous variety in work situations. Some jobs involve close and constant interaction with others while many other jobs can be performed with a much greater degree of independence. Look for work that provides the right balance between external structure and support on the one hand and freedom to do your own thing on the other.

6 **Look for an ADD-friendly work environment.** Look for an environment where your ADD behaviors will be more readily tolerated, for example, (1) where you have more independence, (2) where you are not closely supervised or required to work closely with others, (3) where the atmosphere is more casual, and (4) where the product is more important than the process. Workplace environments that are more casual and less rule-bound are more likely to tolerate aberrations on your part. But remember, no matter where you work—and even if you work only with your spouse—you cannot assume that anything goes and that you don't need to worry about your effect on others. Even the tolerance level of a loyal spouse can be surpassed!

A Final Note on Social Skills

Many adults with ADD have excellent social skills and are drawn into careers that take full advantage of them. Other adults with ADD, those who may experience difficulties and frustration in a corporate environment, are enormously successful in the entrepreneurial world, where they have more freedom, autonomy, and opportunity to create a work world that stimulates and challenges them in positive ways.

Don't become too hard on yourself. Social skills are habits that take repeated practice. With a sense of humor about your foibles, with a genuine desire to get along with others, and perhaps with the assistance of a counselor or therapist, you can make good progress toward improving your on-the-job relationships.

Attention Deficit Disorder is very often associated with other types of cognitive or learning difficulties. This chapter discusses ways to both identify and cope with such problems in adulthood.

ADD and Learning Disabilities

In the ADD Workplace Questionnaire, you are asked to answer a short list of questions under the heading Related Cognitive Difficulties. Answering "yes" to a number of these problems may be an indication that you are dealing with learning disabilities in addition to attentional problems. The presence of these types of cognitive problems is common among people with ADD.[1,2] If they are present, you may benefit from certain types of assistance and from specific types of accommodations on the job.

Why Be Concerned about Learning Disabilities at Work?

The demands of the workplace are constantly changing, and with those technological changes comes the need to continually learn new tasks to keep pace with job requirements. For many of us those changes require us to become computer literate and to learn complicated new software systems. Learning disabilities can have a profound impact on this type of learning. The training that takes place in government, commerce, and industry is not geared, as it is in the academic world, to accommodate the needs of people with learning disabilities.

Until recently, there were many jobs for individuals who had difficulty with reading, writing, and mathematics. The majority of these hands-on jobs have been taken over by machines, and the demands for reading and writing have increased rather than decreased. Thus the need to identify and treat learning problems in adulthood has increased in the past generation.

Learning Anxiety

If you experienced learning difficulties in school, you may be tempted to avoid learning new skills in the workplace, but in today's rapidly changing work world, this approach may severely limit your possibilities for advancement. One of the most difficult aspects of learning for adults with a history of learning problems is the anxiety they experience when they are placed in a situation that reminds them of their school days, that is, where they are expected to read, write, or learn. The following workplace requirements may bring about intense anxiety:

Intensive training workshops

Oral presentations

The requirement to quickly read and respond to written material

Written reports

If you are placed in a new situation that reminds you strongly of frustrating or embarrassing situations from your school years, you may experience a conditioned chain reaction that begins with discomfort, anxiety, or panic and leads to an inability to perform, shame, escape, and lowered self-esteem. Each time you go through a chain reaction like this, your fear of learning or performing is strengthened.

Overcoming Your Learning Anxiety

There are a number of active steps you should undertake if learning anxiety is interfering with work performance.

Let Go of Your Negative Thinking

Many adults today who have learning disabilities were never diagnosed as children and never received any special assistance. They grew up thinking of themselves as poor students or as not very smart.

Now, as more and more adults are being identified with learning problems, centers for adults with learning disabilities are springing up in many cities. Professional educators and tutors are now developing the specialty of working with adults who have learning problems.

Good tutors can help adults with learning disabilities push past their fears and anxieties. When these adults begin to enjoy the challenge of learning and come to believe that they have the ability to improve their skills, they are demonstrating that they have already won more than half the battle. If you don't believe that you can join the ranks of successful learners, take a peek at some of the success stories at the end of this chapter. All of those whose stories I share with you had a long history of academic struggles and failure before they began their learning adventures in adulthood.

Seek an Evaluation of Your Learning Problems

You need to understand exactly what you are dealing with if you have learning problems. More and more adults who were never evaluated for learning problems during childhood are seeking a diagnosis of their difficulties. A good LD evaluation can accomplish the following:

❶ Pinpoint and clarify your specific learning problems

❷ Outline a program to remediate your learning problems

❸ Document your disability, making you eligible for certain types of assistance

There are several national organizations that are dedicated to serving the needs of individuals with learning disabilities. The Learning Disability Association (LDA) is a large national organization that has active chapters in each state. If you are unable to locate your state chapter, call or write LDA (listed in the Resources section at the end of this book) for the address and phone number of your state chapter. Your state chapter should be able to provide you with information about the services and organizations nearest you that offer both testing and follow-up assistance to help you minimize your learning problems.

How to Cope with Learning Problems

Learning disabilities don't go away, but that doesn't mean that there is nothing you can do about them. There are many successful ways to cope with learning problems, including those listed on the following page.

Common Workplace Difficulties for Adults with ADD/LD

There are many different types of difficulties that may be encountered on the job by an adult with both ADD and a learning disability (LD). For more information regarding learning disabilities and workplace functioning, refer to some of the references listed in the Resources section of this book. In the following paragraphs I discuss some of the most common on-the-job difficulties experienced by adults with ADD that may be related to learning disabilities.

Tips for Coping with Learning Problems

☐ **Compensation.** When you compensate for a learning disability, you find a way to work around it. For example, someone with poor mathematical ability may compensate by using a calculator and someone with memory difficulties may compensate for them by writing everything down. A good tutor can teach you compensatory skills.

☐ **Remediation.** When your learning disability is remediated, you have learned methods to actually improve a skill with which you had difficulty. A good tutor who has experience in working with adults can, for example, help people improve their reading or writing abilities.

☐ **Accommodation.** When you are assisted in managing your learning disability, you are said to have been provided accommodations for the disability. Accommodations vary depending on the learning problem. You may be able to provide accommodations for yourself at work, or you may need to request accommodations from your employer. If you have a documented learning disability, you may be eligible to formally request accommodations under the Americans with Disabilities Act (see Chapter 14).

☐ **Talking about your fears.** Many adults with lifelong learning problems have kept them secret out of shame. As you work to overcome your anxiety, it is important that you find understanding and support—from a counselor, a tutor, or another learning disabled adult.

☐ **Seeking or creating supportive learning situations.** If you feel intimidated by an assignment at work, seek help from someone who will be supportive. If a training module at work goes too quickly, tell the trainer you need extra assistance. Ask permission to record training modules in order to review them later. Arrange for extra time to learn

5 LEARNING DISABILITIES

> **Tips for Coping with Learning Problems** *(continued)*
>
> new skills or procedures—even if it means temporarily working in the evening or on weekends. You may need to seek private tutoring to supplement the training you are given on the job. With challenging job assignments it may help to pair up with a coworker whose skills are complementary to yours.
>
> ☐ **Support groups.** Consider joining a support group of learning disabled adults. These groups can provide tremendous reassurance and understanding and are also good sources of information about the resources in your community for learning disabled adults. If your city or town has a center that offers services to adults with learning disabilities, personnel at the center should be able to provide you with information about the existence of local support groups.

Slow Learning Curve

Some ADD adults need significantly more repetitions than non-ADD adults to learn a new task. If you tend to be slow in mastering new material, you will need to take this into account in job selection, avoiding organizations that tend to be pressured and fast paced and choosing one that will allow you to learn naturally, at your own pace. You should be careful not to let yourself be seduced by a higher-paying or more prestigious job whose demands will eventually overwhelm you.

Difficulty in Processing Verbal Information

Prolonged effective listening is a problem for many ADD adults. For some, this is a function of inattention and distractibility. Their ability to concentrate while receiving new information auditorily is limited; attention begins to wander and essential information is missed.

For other ADD adults, listening difficulties are compounded by an auditory processing problem that makes it difficult to receive, process, and comprehend oral input. Because processing spoken language is difficult, they become rapidly fatigued during prolonged meetings, conferences, and intensive training workshops. If an ADD adult has difficulty with prolonged, effective listening, he or she will generally function better doing work that can be done alone or in one-to-one interactive situations. It is also helpful for such an individual to review in advance and in written form any material that will be presented orally; information with which one has some familiarity is easier to process.

Writing Difficulties

Many ADD adults make errors in the mechanics of written language—in spelling, punctuation, capitalization, and grammar—in part because of inattention to detail and impulsivity. The ADD traits of poor planning and organization can also take their toll on writing ability, resulting in reports with run-on sentences, inadequate elaboration, muddled thinking, and poor organization. Many ADD adults who are able to speak articulately find themselves struggling with written expression. Many more skills and abilities come into play when language is expressed in writing.

If writing is a major challenge for you, you should carefully investigate the extent to which writing is required on a job. On the other hand, if your writing difficulties are moderate, you should not automatically eliminate jobs that require writing. Computer programs now minimize the problems associated with the mechanics of writing: The ease with which sentences can be deleted and paragraphs rearranged greatly aids the process of organizing a written document.

Mental Fatigue

Some ADD adults find their energy level rapidly depleted when engaging in any effortful mental activity. One kind of mental fatigue is content specific and is related to an area of learning disability. Another kind occurs with any activity that calls for concentration. ADD adults with this difficulty may be perceived by others as work avoiders owing to their frequent trips away from their desk while they wait for their batteries to recharge. Such individuals often report that they feel tired and sleepy while working but feel energetic as soon as they are up and moving around. For ADD adults who struggle with mental fatigue, a job that allows more physical activity and fewer periods of prolonged concentration is often best.

Whom to Tell about Your Learning Disabilities

The same advice holds for learning disabilities as for ADD (see Chapter 14, ADD and the Americans with Disabilities Act). There is widespread misunderstanding about learning disabilities. An unenlightened employer may hear the term learning disability or LD and assume that you are not capable of performing your job or that you are below average in intellectual ability. The best approach is to find help in the areas where you need it and to ask for accommodations at work, where possible, without making a formal disclosure of your learning disability.[3]

There are circumstances, however, just as with ADD, in which it is to your advantage to disclose your learning disability. Generally, these circumstances are as follows:

 When you have a supportive and sympathetic supervisor who will respond positively to your problem

 When you have tried all other approaches, have found that you cannot do your job effectively without accommodations, and have not been able to obtain those accommodations without a formal disclosure

 When you are in imminent danger of losing your job owing to problems related to your learning disability and feel that with appropriate accommodations you will be able to function well

Back to School with LD and/or ADD

Most of this chapter has focused on the importance of diagnosing and treating learning disabilities because they affect workplace performance. Recognizing and documenting a learning disability is even more essential if you are planning to continue your education. A wide range of services is available to undergraduate, graduate, and professional students who have documented learning disabilities.[4] The documentation required is a learning disability evaluation from a professional qualified to diagnose LD and ADD.

Many adults with learning disabilities or ADD experienced enormous difficulty in their school years and may have quit school as a result. Today their chance for success would be greatly improved. With the support services now available on college campuses, many students with learning problems are completing their college degrees—even medical, law, and graduate degrees.

ADD–LD Success Stories

Many adults with ADD and LD have been able to achieve career success. With the recognition and support that is developing today, the chance of success for someone with ADD and LD is even greater. Let's take a look at several successful adults who have both attentional and learning difficulties. First, a success story from the bad old days, before learning disabilities were understood or accommodations made to them.

Warren is a college graduate and a successful computer specialist in his 40s. He has ADD and learning disabilities. Although highly intelligent in things mechanical and mathematical, he has tremendous difficulty with written expression and with spelling. Warren attended college in the years before there were services for those with learning disabilities on the college level.

During high school Warren had shown tremendous ability and interest in certain activities. For example, he was a gifted amateur photographer and greatly enjoyed working behind the scenes on school plays. His handwriting, however, was almost illegible, and he struggled tremendously with written assignments.

Warren entered a state college where he had the good fortune of meeting a professor who was to become his saving grace. This man, recognizing a real gift in Warren for things logical and systematic, became his mentor, serving as a source of emotional support and as educational advocate. He steered Warren toward professors who required minimal writing and on occasion convinced some of them to reexamine Warren verbally when he failed a written exam. By taking most of his courses in areas with minimal writing requirements and with the support and intervention of this wonderful man, who became a lifelong mentor, Warren was able to graduate from college and achieve tremendous success in the field of computer science.

Warren received no remediation; that is, he received no help to improve his writing difficulties. However, he did receive accommodations—inasmuch as he was able to avoid classes with written requirements and was on occasion permitted to take exams orally. Moreover, he had a mentor who encouraged and believed in him. Finally, he understood his gifts at an early age and chose a field that minimized his disabilities and maximized his strengths.

Now let's take a look at a woman who had struggled all her life with learning disabilities and had assumed she was "stupid."

Frances was a middle-aged woman who had barely graduated from a southern finishing school many years ago. She always had difficulties in school, but her ADD and LD were not diagnosed until she was in her 50s. After many years as a housewife and mother, Frances entered the job market following a divorce, terrified that her age-old problems with learning would emerge again. As a young woman, she had escaped into marriage and motherhood, and until her divorce she had avoided new learning situations as much as possible.

As she began to understand her learning disabilities, Frances began a healing process. While she had always labeled herself stupid, she learned through testing that she had an above-average IQ. Her academic difficulties had been due to memory and oral comprehension problems. In other words, it was difficult for Frances to understand new information when it was presented to her orally (as most new information is!), and she had great difficulty recalling what she had heard.

Armed with this new understanding, and with the ongoing help of a tutor, Frances made major changes in her life. Through her tutor she learned memory improvement techniques. To compensate for her memory problems, she requested written communication at work. She learned the technique of reviewing information in writing to enhance and reinforce oral information, and she learned to habitually take notes whenever information was presented to her orally.

After several months with her tutor, learning ways to remediate and compensate, Frances was a different person on the job—interested, inquisitive, and motivated. She no longer felt that her "stupidity" would soon be discovered, and she had lost much of her fear of learning new information.

Our third success story is about a college graduate who was diagnosed with ADD in middle age, following her teenage daughter's ADD diagnosis. This is the only one of the three success stories presented in this chapter that involves a person who took advantage of the new services available on the college level.

> *Joanne sought an evaluation for ADD when she recognized many of the same behavior patterns in herself that she saw in her daughter, who had recently been diagnosed with ADD. During the course of her evaluation it became clear that learning difficulties, in addition to ADD, had interfered with Joanne's academic functioning during her high school and college years.*
>
> *Although a college graduate, Joanne had a spotty employment record and felt that she had been a failure on many of her jobs. Testing for learning disabilities showed that Joanne had two major areas of difficulty—memory and written language. Like many others with an LD–ADD success story, Joanne learned that her IQ was above average. Her ability to comprehend complex ideas was high, but her ability to memorize and recall detailed information was much lower. Although she had good verbal expressive skills, Joanne had tremendous difficulty organizing her thoughts and putting them into writing.*
>
> *As a result of her testing, Joanne developed the courage to return to school, and with the help of ADD–LD career counseling, she selected the field of social work, where she could take advantage of her gifts of oral expression and could emphasize her strong capacity to understand and work with abstract concepts.*
>
> *To aid her writing difficulty, Joanne began working regularly with a writing tutor, even before her classes in social work began. Although writing will always present a challenge for her,*

(story continued . . .)

now—after working with a tutor for a year—Joanne is earning A's consistently on all of her graduate school papers, is enthusiastic about her future career as a social worker, and no longer considers herself "not very smart."

If You Think You Might Have Learning Disabilities

Too many adults with ADD become overfocused on their ADD and ignore other issues that may be getting in their way. Don't cheat yourself by ignoring possible learning disabilities. If you checked off a number of items on the ADD Workplace Questionnaire relating to cognitive difficulties, you should seek an evaluation from a qualified expert. If the professional who is treating your ADD is not well versed in LD diagnosis and treatment, you may need to work with an LD expert as well. Being diagnosed and receiving treatment for LD is the first crucial step toward taking charge of learning differences that may be limiting your success on the job.[5]

This chapter emphasizes the use of the Myers-Briggs Type Indicator (MBTI) to understand the interaction of personality and ADD and to help adults with ADD make career choices based on their personality type as it interacts with ADD traits.

6

ADD and Personality Type at Work

The Myers-Briggs Type Indicator (MBTI)[1] is a useful tool for assessing basic personality traits and their interaction with ADD. Until recently, very little attention was paid to the MBTI in connection with ADD. Although there is now growing interest in the uses of the MBTI with ADD, only limited research has been undertaken. What is written in this chapter is based on my clinical experience over the past several years, in administering the MBTI to individuals during both assessment for ADD and as a part of ongoing treatment for adult ADD.

This chapter describes how your personality preferences, as measured by the MBTI, interact with ADD and emphasizes how a knowledge of your MBTI personality type can be essential to understanding your ADD behaviors in the workplace, to formulating an appropriate treatment approach, and, to making wise career decisions.

ADD is *Not* a Personality Type!

Just as people with ADD come in all shapes and sizes, they also come in all personality types. In reading descriptions of individuals with ADD, it is tempting to conclude that ADD is a personality type, that people with ADD are very active, talkative, impulsive, creative, and terribly disorganized. These adjectives describe some adults with ADD, but anyone who has worked with adults with ADD knows that there is tremendous variation among them. You may have had the experience of reading books on ADD that described you to a tee. These books are describing the ADD traits that many adults with ADD have in common, traits you recognize in yourself. It is important to realize, however, that such books narrowly address ADD and ignore equally important non-ADD personality traits.

Because we are still in the early stages of understanding and working with adults who have ADD, the variations among them, caused by differences in personality type, have been all but ignored. Some adults with ADD are talkative extroverts while others are quiet and private. Some are hyperactive, others are virtual couch potatoes. Some are highly impulsive while others tend to be vague and indecisive. Some are highly intellectual, but many others disliked school and gravitated toward more active pursuits. What all these people share in common is some combination of core symptoms of ADD. This chapter will emphasize individual personality differences among people with ADD and will discuss how those differences interact with certain ADD traits to influence work functioning.

Although your ADD symptoms may play a very strong role in your life, you are much more complex than a list of ADD symptoms. By taking a measure of your personality traits and thinking about them in combination with your ADD, you will have a more complete picture of your strengths, weaknesses, interests, and preferences. Taking all of these factors into account, you will be much better able to find a good job or career match for yourself.

A Brief Description of the MBTI

I have used the Myers-Briggs Type Indicator (MBTI) as a measure of personality type for several reasons. It is brief, widely available, and inexpensive to administer, and it has been studied extensively in relation to job satisfaction and career match.[2] The MBTI is also preferable to many other psychological tests of personality because it measures personality preferences in a nonjudgmental fashion, emphasizing personality preferences, not problems.

The MBTI was developed based on the personality theory of the well-known psychoanalyst Carl Jung, who believed that individuals have certain inborn traits that form the basic building blocks of their personality.[3] Jung believed that these traits are fundamental and lifelong but that they can develop and change in certain respects. Interestingly, as neuroscientists learn more about the neurobiological basis for personality traits, we are now beginning to see scientific evidence to support Jung's belief that people are born with different personalities.

Understanding MBTI "Preferences"

According to the MBTI people vary according to four pairs of "preferences":

Extroverted (E) or Introverted (I)

Sensing (S) or Intuitive (N)

Thinking (T) or Feeling (F)

Judging (J) or Perceiving (P)

Let's take a look at each of these eight preferences in order to understand how they are defined according to the MBTI.[4]

Extroversion versus Introversion

Extroverts (E's) are people who are energized by interaction with others and actively seek their company. Being around people is life's blood for the extrovert. People who are strongly extroverted may feel lonely and isolated when forced to engage in solitary activities. They often prefer verbal over written communication, and they seek discussions with others in making decisions. They tend to relate to a broad range of people instead of maintaining only a few in-depth relationships.

Whereas extroverts are social and are oriented toward the external world—they live in a world of "we"—introverts (I's) inhabit a more private, internal world. Introverts tend to recharge, or reenergize, themselves in isolation from others. Social interaction, especially with groups or with people who are not intimates, is energy draining for introverts. Although a certain amount of interaction is necessary within the course of a day, introverts are prone to close the office door, to wish the meeting were over, to turn off the telephone, and to want to leave the party early. Their energy level becomes depleted after prolonged interaction with others.

Different Problem-Solving Styles

Introverts and extroverts differ in problem-solving style. Introverts are drawn more toward activities that require narrow focus and concentration. They are prone to turn inward when making a decision and to announce their decision to others after they have reached their own conclusion. Even when engaged in problem solving with others, an introvert is likely to mull things over before discussing the matter. By contrast, many extroverts begin to develop their ideas as they engage in discussion and dialogue with others. For extroverts, the very act of communicating with others often sparks ideas that haven't yet occurred to them.

Cultural Bias Toward Extroverts

In the United States, in particular, there seems to be a strong cultural bias toward extroversion. (Introverts not only have to face this social bias against their type but also find themselves outnumbered 3 to 1 in the general population.) Introverts may be seen as withdrawn or lacking in social skills. Because of this cultural preference, many introverts (intentionally or not) try to respond to the MBTI as if they were extroverts. In fact, many introverts spend most of their lives attempting to behave in an extroverted fashion, trying to suppress introverted tendencies.

For example, one business executive who answered the MBTI as an extrovert protested when his examiner suggested that he was more likely an introvert; he insisted that he was seen as a genial, outgoing person at work. This "I in E clothing" made the mistake many people do, namely, confusing extroversion with social skills. Like many introverts, he had developed excellent social skills. He was well liked and was highly regarded as an executive. Unlike a true extrovert, however, he tended to yearn for time when he could close his office door to get some work done and he typically spent his evenings in quiet isolation to recover from his energy-draining people-filled day.

6 PERSONALITY TYPE

Appreciating the Powers of Introversion

If you are an introvert, understand your "I" tendencies and celebrate them! Don't try to join the E's of the world in the erroneous assumption that introversion is something to change or hide. I's who try to force themselves into the shoes of an E won't enjoy walking and will probably get blisters! Accepting your introversion will lead to a much more satisfactory choice of career. It is the I's of the world who are able to sit and focus in order to write, create, learn, invent, and accomplish.

**An extrovert
uses his answering machine
to catch calls while he's out.
An introvert
uses his answering machine
to screen calls when he's in.**

Sensing versus Intuition

Just as the majority of people are extroverts, most (approximately 75% of the population) have a preference for sensation as opposed to a preference for intuition.[5] Those who prefer sensation, the S's, live in the world of real, touchable, practical things whereas those who prefer intuition, the N's, live in the domain of ideas and innovations. Another way to express this difference is to say that S's live in the world of the actual while N's focus on possibilities.

S's Emphasize Hands-On Experience

S's place the strongest emphasis on their experience, on what has actually happened. The nickname for Missouri—the "Show Me" State—must have been inspired by a group of S's! Just like Missourians, S's want to be shown the actual proof of things. They trust their own experience and pay the greatest attention to their surroundings, noticing details, collecting facts, and making concrete plans. Because S's live in the world of things, they are natural-born shoppers. An S will likely read the newspaper ads for sales and will be the best source of information on where something can be bought for the best price.

N's Live in the World of Ideas

N's, on the other hand, live intuitively; they think of grand schemes, of possibilities, of the future. N's are attuned to the creative, the imagined, the not yet actual. For an S, the N's of the world may seem a bit flighty and impractical, dreamers who are always off in the clouds, who ignore the day-to-day requirements of life. N's in turn may view S's as unimaginative, plodding, and aware only of the boring, repetitive daily grind.

S's and N's Form a Powerful Team

S's often make good planners and managers; they pay attention to the details of what has occurred and what needs to be taken care of next. N's make good creators, visionaries. A company with an N at the helm will always be moving toward the future, developing innovations, seeking new markets, and expanding in unexpected directions. The actual execution of these grand schemes is best carried out by S's, however. A company with an S at the helm will be more solid and practical, with an eye on the bottom line and on competitors, but with little sense of direction other than an impulse to continue to do whatever it has done best in the past.

Of all the contrasts between personality preferences, the S–N difference is considered the greatest. It is almost as if S's and N's speak different languages and have difficulty in translating from one to the other. However, if this translation succeeds—if the two can learn to work together, respecting and understanding their differences—an S and an N can prove to be an unbeatable team!

An N expands life's possibilities.
An S makes the possible actual.

Thinking versus Feeling

Thinkers (T's) approach decisions from a detached, analytical, logical position. They value justice perhaps more highly than compassion. Feelers (F's), on the other hand, make decisions in a more subjective manner, that is, by responding with empathy and trying to consider extenuating circumstances. For example, when someone has broken a rule, a T is likely to impose a standard penalty whereas an F would, as if by reflex, consider the circumstances that led to the infraction. The T might say, "He has to pay the price for what he has done," but an F might add, "Yes, but he's never done anything like this before, and he was under tremendous stress when this happened."

Gender Differences

This thinker–feeler dichotomy is the only set of preferences that shows a slight gender-related bias: Approximately 60% of women are F's whereas approximately 60% of men are T's.[6] T's and F's can work together with great complementarity inasmuch as good decision making requires that both the thinking and the feeling aspects of a question be considered. Of course, we are all capable of considering both T and F aspects of questions, but people generally tend to have a preference in one direction or the other.

People versus Production

Both T's and F's are capable of experiencing strong emotional reactions to events, but since F's are more likely to openly show their emotions, they are usually seen as warmer and more compassionate than T's. The higher one goes in the management hierarchy of an organization, the more likely one is to be a T. It may be that T qualities are necessary to guard the interests of the organization against the multiple competing needs of the employees. The T keeps an ever-vigilant eye on the bottom line. It may be just as true, however, that Fs are rare in upper management jobs because such positions of leadership, which are so detached from personal involvement with people, are not attractive to them.

**T's think with their head.
F's think with their heart.**

Judging versus Perceiving

The words judging and perceiving can be easily misinterpreted. It is a common error to think that "judging" means "to be judgmental." A better way of distinguishing judgers (J's) from perceivers (P's) is to think of the difference between "defined" and "open-ended." J's are result oriented and seem to have a work ethic. They want to get the job done, to make a plan, to meet the deadline. P's, on the other hand, have more of a play ethic. They don't see the same value or urgency in accomplishing work. They feel much more strongly that work should be enjoyable, and they are likely to seek ways to avoid those tasks that are not enjoyable.

Deadlines

One of the most observable differences between J's and P's can be seen in their responses to deadlines. For J's, a deadline is a serious limit that should be met. J's meet deadlines and expect their coworkers to meet them as well. For P's, a deadline is seen as more of a marker that can slide. For some P's, a deadline can even be seen as a signal to begin a project rather than a time to complete it! (This P preference can easily be mistaken for the procrastination patterns found in adults with ADD. However, there is an important difference: Whereas P's prefer to operate in that fashion, many adults with ADD feel almost helpless to work against their tendency to procrastinate and feel frustrated by the pattern.)

Decisions

Another major difference can be found in decision making. J's, who like order, plans, and closure, tend to feel a sense of unease or agitation until a decision is made. "Let's figure out what we're going to do and make a decision," a J would say. Once a decision is made, the J feels more relaxed and secure. This drive or sense of urgency to make decisions or to settle issues can sometimes lead to decisions that are made too quickly, without gathering enough information. P's, by contrast, have a great tolerance for ambiguity and are quite comfortable considering all aspects of a question. P's are always happy to wait before making a decision. "Who knows? Perhaps new options will emerge that I didn't recognized earlier," a P would say. Whereas a J feels relief after a decision is made, this type of closure often causes the opposite reaction in a P. "If we decide now, we may be closing off other options that could be better," a P would argue. "Why don't we just keep thinking, talking, and gathering information a bit longer?"

**J's want plans to come together.
P's want plans to hang loose.**

MBTI Types and Mistyping

In order for this chapter to be most useful for you, you will need to obtain an accurate measure of your MBTI personality type. You may have already taken the MBTI. Several million people take the MBTI each year! If you have taken it, the primary concern is whether you received an accurate measure of your type. If you are correctly typed, the MBTI can be enormously informative and useful in considering career concerns.

The reader should be aware that it is quite possible to take the MBTI and receive incorrect results. One man spoke with great mistrust of the MBTI, saying that he had taken it several times and had received a different personality type each time. How is this possible? The MBTI is not magic. It is simply a way of organizing and interpreting your responses. "Garbage in, garbage out" is the rule that applies here. To be typed correctly, you must answer questions according to your true preferences, not according to how you think you ought or are required to behave and not according to your mood of the moment. People may be typed incorrectly if they have a job or lifestyle that requires them to behave very differently than they would naturally choose to behave. To be accurately typed, you must respond to the MBTI according to your true inclinations, even though the demands of your daily life may require you to behave otherwise.

Mistyping in the Business World

People who take the MBTI as part of a workplace exercise may consciously or unconsciously answer questions in accordance with the values of the institution or in response to perceived social pressures. For example, some people in the business world may feel pressured to behave in an extroverted fashion even though by nature they are more private. Moreover, men in general (and perhaps especially those in the business world) may feel a strong social pressure to be logical rather than emotional. Thus, men who are truly "feelers" may respond to questions on the MBTI in a way that types them as "thinkers," just as true introverts may respond in a way that types them as extroverts. Moreover, as women make efforts to reach upper-level management, those who are "feelers" may also be tempted to misrepresent themselves as "thinkers."

Mistyping in Periods of Personal Change

Another source of mistyping can occur when a person is in counseling or is going through a midlife crisis, a divorce, a career change, or any other major life transition. These are all generally situations of internal turmoil and change. During such times people may try to "become" different. As they experiment with different ways of feeling and responding, they may answer the MBTI accordingly.

Do Personality Types Change?

According to Jungian theory, our basic personality preferences are inborn and don't change throughout our lifetime.[7] This does not mean that we cannot make changes or improvements in ourselves. In fact, many people in their middle years begin to develop other aspects of their personality. For example, extroverts may begin to develop their introverted side by taking up more solitary activities. Thinkers who have spent their careers focusing on the impersonal world of things may begin to learn how to express their emotions more openly. These changes are very healthy and result in a more balanced life, but they don't result in a basic change in personality type. The situation is a bit like that of right-handed people who learn to eat with their left hands; although they can learn to do it, they will continue to have a strong preference for their right hands.

Learning Your MBTI Type

The best way to be typed is to take the MBTI by a trained professional who can score and interpret the results for you. If you are currently in counseling, your psychotherapist or counselor may be able to administer the test. If such testing is not readily available, however, there are short forms of the MBTI in a number of books written on the subject. You can find these books listed in the Resources section at the end of this book.

MBTI Preferences versus ADD Tendencies

There is an important distinction to be made between the traits measured by the MBTI, which are personality preferences, and the symptoms associated with ADD. When Carl Jung developed his theory of personality, he attempted to describe the inborn personal preferences of individuals. According to Jung, each individual is born with these preferences and is most natural and comfortable in life when he or she behaves in accordance with those preferences. This set of preferences should not be confused with behavior patterns or tendencies associated with ADD. ADD traits are not due to personal preferences. They are the result of neurobiological factors (i.e., neurochemical and perhaps structural differences in the brain) that make certain cognitive processes much more difficult. For example, a person can have a strong tendency to stutter, but he or she is unlikely to have a preference for stuttering. The same kind of distinction can be made for many ADD traits.

Some professionals who are knowledgeable about the Myers-Briggs personality types but who are not experts in ADD sometimes confuse preferences and tendencies. For example, among certain MBTI personality types there are individuals whose preference is to be active and impulsive with little tolerance for detailed, mundane work. Such a person might be mistaken for one with ADD. In fact, there are those who mistakenly believe that ADD is a personality type rather than a neurobiological disorder. In a study of several hundred schoolchildren, however, the MBTI personality types that might be mistaken for ADD were found slightly more often among non-ADD students than among those with ADD![8]

Although people with ADD come in all personality types, it is certainly possible for them to have personality preferences that are consistent with certain ADD traits. When personality preferences and ADD tendencies coincide, the result is an intensification of both! Double trouble!

**ADD strategies
must fit your personality**

When MBTI Preferences Combine with ADD

I have discussed the eight MBTI preferences without regard to ADD. In this section I will attempt to examine the ways that MBTI preferences interact with ADD patterns, focusing in particular on the ways they interact in the workplace environment.

Extroverts (E's) with ADD

The hyperactivity of an adult ADD extrovert is likely to be manifested by hypersociability. It's likely that he or she was the schoolchild who was constantly talking in class. For the hyperactive, extroverted adult, people are likely to be one of life's major distractions. Extroverts (E's) are drawn to people to recharge, to discuss, and to problem-solve. When an E is also ADD, these discussions are likely to wander off the track, extend in time, and lose their effectiveness.

Problems with Isolation

Solutions for ADD-related problems need to be modified according to MBTI preferences. For example, one man, an E with ADD, was highly distracted by conversations and by people walking by in the hall near his office. His therapist suggested that he shut his office door periodically to decrease these distractions. Because the man was such a strong E, this solution was unworkable for him. With his door shut he found that his productivity became even worse! He felt isolated and was so curious about the bits and snatches of conversation he could overhear through his closed door that these conversations became even more distracting than before. A much more effective solution for him was to "time-shift" his hours. He began arriving at work at 7:30 A.M., which allowed him an hour or more of uninterrupted time to do paperwork, check e-mail, and organize his day before his coworkers began arriving.

Hyperverbalizing

E's with ADD need to guard against hyperverbalization. One man who sold technical equipment found that his major problem in sales was talking his client's ear off. He made some progress in checking this tendency by making brief notes of the points he wanted to make before calling each client. For initial calls he developed a script that helped keep him on track but with which he allowed himself some latitude. He also used timers for himself and set the goal of limiting client calls to 10 minutes.

Need to Work with People

E's who have unwittingly acquired jobs more suited to introverts (I's) may tend to prolong meetings, to socialize at the water fountain, and to infringe on the time of others because of their hunger for interaction. Those with ADD are even more likely to become caught up in such nonproductive behavior and may be misperceived by their boss or coworkers as "goof-offs." If you find that these are your tendencies, you should consider shifting to a job that requires people interaction. This same energy and drive to socialize, which can be seen as work avoidance in some jobs, can benefit you greatly in a people-oriented job.

Introverts (I's) with ADD

What happens when ADD is combined with introversion? One of the risks is that the preference of introverts (I's) to be alone will conflict with the ADD need for external structure. If a person with ADD is isolated for significant portions of each day, it is quite easy as for him or her to drift off the track and not realize that this has taken place. One introvert (I) with ADD learned to cue himself to keep on track. He set goals for himself at the beginning of each day and estimated an approximate time period for each task. He then found it helpful to set a timer to sound every half hour as a cue to check his focus and his progress.

Prefer to Communicate in Writing

E-mail is a wonderful invention for I's. One I with ADD found that it was helpful to communicate frequently with his boss by e-mail as a means of building structure and receiving feedback. He set weekly goals for himself and sent them to his boss (down the hall) by e-mail. At the end of each week he e-mailed his boss a progress report. They met face-to-face twice monthly. E-mail allowed him to minimize direct interaction but, at the same time, to benefit from external structure and guidance.

Stress Sensitive

I's report that they frequently feel overwhelmed by too many interruptions or too much verbal interaction. They become flooded or overwhelmed with stimulation to the point that they shut down. Again, e-mail can provide a solution to such flooding, because it can allow efficient communication without overloading the verbal interaction circuits. Some I's with ADD have carefully arranged to work at night to avoid overstimulation. One I with ADD, who was very sensitive to stress and overstimulation, arranged his workday so that he could arrive home before rush hour and complete phone calls and paperwork from the peace and quiet of his home.

Sensers (S's) with ADD

What happens when those who prefer sensation (S's) have ADD? S's are practical, active, and focused on the world of things. An S with ADD may be especially prone to start far too many projects and to constantly find him- or herself in the middle of incompleted renovations and repairs. An S with ADD may shop compulsively or may pick up many hobbies, which they drop as they pursue their next interest. They are likely to buy all the latest equipment for each new hobby, only to leave all these acquisitions in disarray as they move on to something else.

Surrounded by "Things"

How does the combination of ADD and this trait translate into the workplace? The same patterns can be found at work: a tendency toward great physical disorder, toward the acquisition of too many things, and toward impulsive spending and unrealistic budgeting. S's with ADD are the inventors of the world; they are constantly tinkering, building, adding on. These tendencies can be a great asset if they are managed, but all too often S's with ADD live surrounded by objects in midcompletion or midrepair.

Lost in the Details

S's with ADD may be especially prone to become lost in the details of a project. For example, one man decided to make improvements in the daytimer system he used to help him plan and organize. He became completely engrossed in this project, developing special color coding systems, huge computer printouts, and intricate systems of symbols, meanwhile never putting his time-management program into effect.

S's with ADD often need a non-ADD colleague to help them reach closure. When they are teamed with someone who can provide boundaries and limits their practical solutions can be quite creative and valuable to the organization.

Intuitives (N's) with ADD

People who prefer intuition (N's) and who also have ADD have the potential to be among the most creative and prolific people in the world—if their energy and interests can be harnessed. N's live in the world of theories, ideas, and innovations. Unlike the innovations of their S counterparts, the innovations of N's are not of the concrete "build a better mousetrap" variety but are more likely to concern the abstract themes of art, philosophy, educational theory, or government policy. N's with ADD often report that they live with a flood of ideas and associations and that they tend to be highly distracted by their own internal world.

Drowning in a Sea of Ideas

One N with severe ADD, a highly intelligent man, reported with enormous frustration that he wanted to write a book for others like himself but found that he couldn't organize and develop his thoughts. Although he had developed a huge list of random thoughts and associations over the course of several years of intense effort, he was unable to combine these into a format he could communicate to others. Another N with ADD, a man whose organizational problems were less severe, described his professional life as very satisfying but constantly stressful. He found that he was interested in a huge range of topics and was unable to realistically assess the demands of his current commitments before taking on another tempting project. As an adult with ADD he also struggled with procrastination and invariably put off papers and reports until the last minute.

Visionaries in Need of a Plan

In the workplace, N's can be great leaders and visionaries. However, an N with ADD at the helm of an organization is likely to lead the entire organization into his or her world of unrealistic plans, over-commitment, and frequent crises created by poor planning and procrastination. Team up such an N with a non-ADD S, and many more of his or her ideas will bear fruit!

Thinkers (T's) with ADD

When ADD occurs in those whose preferred style is for thinking over feeling (the T's), the result is sometimes a combination of troubling interpersonal tendencies. Thinkers (T's) prefer to deal with non-people issues: technology, profit, efficiency, or procedure. Their emotional, empathic side is much less developed. While some T's may be good observers of human reactions, they are not prone to respond in a fashion that engenders closeness or understanding. Many people with ADD also have difficulty in reading social cues and emotional responses. It is as if their engine is running so fast (i.e., they are so preoccupied with their own thoughts and activities) that there is little time or energy left over to expend on people. When a thinking preference is combined with ADD, problems with people skills can be doubly intensified.

Missing Social Cues

When ADD traits of impatience and low frustration tolerance are combined with a T's lack of attention to the feelings of others, there may be significant interpersonal problems on the job. Such people may be both difficult to work for and difficult to manage or supervise. If they are extroverts, they may be especially prone to talk nonstop and to be oblivious to the effect they are having on others. If they are introverts, their attempts to escape from the demands of interpersonal interaction may make them respond to people in a way that suggests indifference or annoyance.

Need to Build Social Skills

Social skills are likely to be a major difficulty for T's with ADD. They will do well to team themselves closely with an F who can temper their reactions and can give them feedback about their effect on coworkers.

Feelers (F's) with ADD

Feelers (F's) with ADD are in a better position to develop good social skills. While T's with ADD have a doubly influenced tendency to misread or overlook social cues, F's with ADD have a tendency to be tuned in to the needs and feelings of others. This tendency gives F's with ADD the means to counteract some of the interpersonal problems sometimes caused by ADD. For example, F's with ADD may still blurt out something in a blunt or undiplomatic fashion. Their built-in social radar, however, will quickly tell them that they have overstepped the bounds of considerate behavior, thus giving them an opportunity to apologize and to "mend fences." One woman, an F with ADD, reported that she was always having to "sweep up the pieces" after she had unintentionally upset someone. In fact, she consciously developed a charming, self-deprecating, and outgoing manner in order to compensate for unintentional faux pas.

Emotionality

F's with ADD may find that their emotional and interpersonal reactions are intense, because their ADD traits toward overemotionality combine with their emotional sensitivity. Whereas a T with ADD may have fairly thick skin and may be somewhat oblivious to the negative reactions of others, F's with ADD, by contrast, are likely not only to be aware of others' hurt feelings but to experience such feelings themselves. Some F's with ADD (more often female, though not always) may feel that they are on an emotional roller coaster, with strong tendencies toward tears, anxiety, and depression.

Intense Relationships

The emotional intensity of F's with ADD in combination with their social sensitivity may also lead them to have intense intimate friendships and love relationships. This is in marked contrast to T's with ADD (more often male), who may be emotionally unavailable and may have relatively few relationships with others. F's with ADD, if well matched to their careers and jobs, can use their strong awareness of others to advantage, in sales, public relations, and in any other type of work requiring people interaction and sensitivity. Stress can be the Achilles' heel for F's with ADD. During high stress their heightened sensitivity to others may lead to overreactions and less effective functioning.

Judgers (J's) with ADD

Judgers (J's) with ADD are in a battle with themselves. Owing to their strong preference for order, closure, and predictability, J's tend to be frustrated by their ADD. The disorganization caused by their ADD is at odds with their built-in preference for order. Their battle has both positive and negative consequences. If the resulting frustration is extreme, it can result in self-rejection, low self-esteem, and depression. If the frustration is mild, it can result in the development of effective coping techniques.

Tendency Toward Rigidity

In extreme cases, J's with ADD may develop patterns that can be misunderstood as obsessive-compulsive tendencies. In their attempt to gain control over their uncooperative ADD brains, J's may develop numerous rituals and habits to which they adhere rigidly. When J tendencies and ADD traits are both strong, the degree of rigidity may become extreme, causing problems for the J in living and working with others.

Compensate Well for ADD

When J tendencies are less pronounced or when the ADD traits are less severe, J's with ADD have a great advantage over P's in compensating for ADD patterns. Often, even without the assistance of others, J's naturally develop behavior patterns or habits consisting of techniques to combat absentmindedness, to cope with distractions, to stay on schedule, to meet deadlines, and so on. Typically, J's with ADD eagerly adopt all the coping techniques that come to their attention, since suggestions to create and maintain order are highly compatible with their own internal drives. These drives constitute their great strength: If they can moderate their frustration and their negative evaluation of themselves when their ADD breaks through, J's have a great capacity and desire to compensate for their ADD.

Perceivers (P's) with ADD

Perceivers (P's), on the other hand, can suffer from what might seem like an excess of comfort with their ADD! ADD patterns may be more irritating and troubling for those who live and work with P's with ADD than for the P's with ADD themselves! This is because P's (with or without ADD) by nature prefer to live in a less ordered, defined, predictable fashion. When their natural preference for spur-of-the-moment living is combined with the impulsivity of ADD, a volatile combination can result. Unlike J's with ADD, P's have no brakes—only accelerators. Thus, P's with ADD may feel it is entirely justified to change plans at the last moment if they have just been inspired by a new idea or motivated by an impulse to do something more desirable. Their surroundings are likely to reflect the fact that they live at the highest level of chaos, with little or no organization among their papers and belongings.

Need for a Tolerant Environment

P's with ADD may experience more difficulty than other personality types in finding a workplace environment that can tolerate their disorganization and appreciate their gifts. One P with ADD, for this very reason, started his own small advertising agency. Being the boss, he answered to no one. When his assistant arrived promptly at 8:30 each morning, she often found her boss asleep on the carpet, where he had crashed after working all night. Similarly, after working nonstop on a project, he felt free to take a day or two off, even midweek. By working for himself he was able to create a work life that was compatible with his strong P tendencies to follow the ebb and flow of his energies.

Need for Help with Structure

While P's with ADD can be tremendously creative, effective people, they (perhaps more than other ADD adults) have great need of organized non-ADD persons to help them maintain some degree of order in their work lives.

MBTI Personality Types

Through combining the eight basic preferences described in this chapter, the MBTI classifies a person according to sixteen personality types:

ISTJ	ISFJ	INFJ	INTJ
ISTP	ISFP	INFP	INTP
ESTP	ESFP	ENFP	ENTP
ESTJ	ESFJ	ENFJ	ENTJ

I have talked in broad strokes about the eight preferences of the MBTI* and how these preferences may interact with ADD. In reality, however, the picture is far more complex than this. Each person has four preferences, which interact with one another. ADD traits complicate the issue even further. For example, an extroverted P with a preference toward feelings and an introverted P who is a logical, analytical thinker are going to be affected by their ADD very differently.

It is far beyond the scope of this chapter—it could indeed be a book in itself—to talk of each personality type and its potential interaction with ADD. There are many excellent books written on the subject of the Myers-Briggs Type Indicator, some of which are listed in the Resources section of this book. Reading these books, especially those with a focus on the MBTI and careers, and thinking of the ways that personality type and ADD interact, which I have only touched upon in this chapter, can be helpful to you in making career choices or changes.

The most important message to take from this chapter is that you are much more than an adult with ADD. It's certainly very important to be aware of ADD traits and tendencies, but don't lose sight of the fact that you are unique and complex. Solutions to your ADD problems need to be custom-tailored to you, taking your personality preferences into consideration. Keeping your personality preferences in mind, in combination with ADD issues, will help you make a choice that makes sense for you, not just for your ADD!

6 PERSONALITY TYPE

---

*Note: In several subsequent chapters you will find many references to aspects of the MBTI. If you are not familiar with the MBTI, you may find it helpful to refer back to this chapter and to read some of the books on the MBTI listed in the Resources section at the end of this book.

The preceding chapters emphasize the potential problems caused by ADD at work. This chapter attempts to balance the scale a bit by talking about the potentially positive side of ADD.

Putting the Positive Side of ADD to Work

The chances are that you are reading this book because ADD has led to difficulties for you in the workplace. It is extremely important, however, not to lose track of the potentially positive side of ADD. There are many adults with ADD who have been enormously successful in life despite their ADD—indeed, in many respects, because of their ADD. That's right, because of it! There is an upside to ADD for many people. As is true for the downside of ADD, people differ with respect to the positive ADD traits they possess. It's important that you make a realistic assessment of yourself. If you can recognize your positive ADD traits and learn how to take advantage of them, you can make the best choices about where to put those positive traits to work.

The Positive Side of ADD

Just what are the positive aspects of ADD? Most of what has been written about ADD emphasizes areas of *dys*function. If you travel within the community of ADD adults, however, you will encounter a different story. The following page shows a list of positive traits associated with ADD adults, a list that was developed by an adult ADD support group:

The "Up" Side of ADD	
Creative	Good in a crisis
Resilient	Able to hyperfocus on projects
Energetic	Love a challenge
Enthusiastic	Love to interact with people
Determined	Good at communicating
Can think "on their feet"	Seek variety and stimulation

How many of these traits do you have? Studying this list may be a starting point for you in putting your ADD to work for you!

Redefining Negative ADD Traits

The list above was developed expressly to emphasize the positive side of ADD. As an exercise in positive thinking, let's go back to the list of symptoms of ADD and consider the upside of these "dysfunctions."

Distractible or Superobservant?

Another way to describe those who are distractible is to say that they are highly observant. Their attention is attracted by the most minute change in the environment. This trait is part of the set of hunter traits described by Thom Hartmann in his book *Attention Deficit Disorder: A Different Perception.*[1] One woman with ADD used her visual distractability to great advantage in the restaurant she owned and managed with her husband. Her energy and hypervigilance led her to automatically notice the smallest detail and kept her fine-dining restaurant running smoothly.

Internal Distractions or Rich Imagination?

Many individuals with ADD enjoy a rich imagination. They make rapid and unique associations between different facts and fields. Often such individuals find that their best ideas come to them when they are working on something else entirely. If you can learn to harness this wonderful creativity by recording and later returning to your ideas, you have turned this "deficit" into a marvelous strength. One renowned scientist who was diagnosed with ADD reported that this rapid flow of ideas and associations was his greatest asset as a scientist.

Hyperfocusing or Enormous Capacity to Concentrate?

Many successful people take great advantage of their tendency to hyperfocus. People from any field that calls upon concentrated, creative thought—writers, musicians, computer experts, designers, engineers, scientists—are at an enormous advantage if they are able to hyperfocus for long hours while working.

Impulsive or Capable of Quick Responses?

Impulsive people are quick reactors. Often they are more effective than reflective people in situations that call for quick action. For example, one ADD adult has developed a highly successful career in California as a free-lance television journalist. He has capitalized on his quick, impulsive style. He listens to the radio and to the police radio throughout the day. He has a history of being the first one on the spot with the best film footage of a newsworthy event. Impulsive people are more likely to seize the moment, take the chance, make the sale, grab the opportunity.

Hyperactivity or High Energy Level?

Hyperactivity and restlessness can also be seen as having high energy—a tremendously positive trait if you can find appropriate outlets for it. Many high-energy people become entrepreneurs, a lifestyle that allows them to take full advantage of their high energy level and that gives them the freedom to minimize activities that are sedentary.

Inattention to Detail or Capacity to See the Big Picture?

"Big picture" people can make tremendous contributions to an organization. They often have vision and are highly motivated to come up with new programs and procedures. Whether you are in a large organization or are creating your own entrepreneurial enterprise, you can put such traits to your advantage.

Easily Bored or Tremendous Capacity for Innovation?

So many people with ADD are described as easily bored—as if that were a negative trait that they would be so much better off without! But intolerance of the mundane and routine can lead to enormous creativity and innovation.

An ADD Perspective on the Rest of the World

One of the most important messages in Thom Hartmann's book *Attention Deficit Disorder: A Different Perception* is how the negative definition of ADD can be turned on its head. Hartmann describes adults with ADD as "hunters" and non-ADD adults as "farmers." He emphasizes the positive aspects of these hunters and underlines their tremendous potential and actual contributions to our society.

Since ADD has been so negatively defined by the "farmers" of our society, as an exercise in fair play let's describe the "farmer" from the perspective of "hunters." We might, for example, say that the "farmer" suffers from Attention-Excess Disorder, whose symptoms are as follows:

7 POSITIVE SIDE

"Attention Excess Disorder"
Prefers following established routines
Moderate-to-low energy level
Low tolerance for change or ambiguity
Low tolerance for risk
Limited capacity to respond quickly in crisis situations
Slow, laborious decision making
Limited capacity to find novel solutions
Tends to think in a linear fashion
Processes and interprets incoming stimuli slowly

Any set of patterns and tendencies can be described in an exaggeratedly negative way. Obviously, there are advantages and disadvantages to being either a "hunter" with Attention Deficit Disorder, or a "farmer" with "Attention Excess Disorder." The important message for adults with ADD is not to buy into the "farmer's" view of ADD. People, with or without ADD, have both strengths and weaknesses. The important issue is to understand those positives and negatives and to place yourself where your talents and abilities are most likely to thrive.

Going Overboard on the Positive ADD Perspective

Both Thom Hartmann and Ned Hallowell,[2] a psychiatrist and ADD adult himself, have placed a tremendous emphasis on the positive side of ADD. In fact, the positive emphasis of both writers has stirred debate in the ADD community. Some feel that Hartmann and Hallowell have almost ignored the serious struggles of adults with ADD by too strongly emphasizing the positive. They fear that ADD has been trivialized and that efforts to better understand this disorder and to develop improved treatment approaches for it will not receive the time, attention, and badly needed research dollars.

Both authors describe adults with ADD who are not severely affected and who have the capacity to succeed in spite of (and even because of) ADD traits. Hartmann clearly states that his intention is to write about and for those adults with ADD who have above-average intelligence and ability. He leaves to other writers the task of addressing the needs of the more severely affected sector of the ADD population.

Keep a Balanced View

The important issue for you, as an adult with ADD, is to recognize that there are positive aspects to ADD. By only focusing on the problem side of ADD, you are less likely to appreciate your abilities. With a balanced view of yourself, you are better prepared to make good career choices.

Successful People with ADD

Because ADD in adults is so newly recognized, there is no list of well-known adults who have been diagnosed with ADD, but quite a number of famous people have been nominated as "ADD successes" on the basis of their known traits and behaviors.[3] Among them are John Kennedy, Thomas Edison, Nelson Rockefeller, Bill Clinton, Winston Churchill, Benjamin Franklin, and Robin Williams.

The worlds of politics, comedy, music, athletics, sales, television, and entrepreneurial enterprises are likely places to look for successful ADD adults. Does this mean that you should try to head in those directions? Not necessarily! Those ADD adults who are successes in these fields have a very lucky combination of talent, intelligence, and certain ADD traits, a combination that can be dynamite.

7 POSITIVE SIDE

Since most of us aren't headed for fame, it is probably more helpful to focus on more "ordinary" ADD adults who have become successful. These are not adults who have world-class looks, musical ability, or athletic skills but, rather, people who, by luck or good judgment, put themselves in circumstances that have allowed them to soar. Let's look at people of different ages and educational and social backgrounds who have succeeded because of their positive ADD traits. In each of these stories I have used pseudonyms in order to protect the privacy of the individuals involved. The circumstances of their lives have been altered only in ways to protect their privacy, but the important and essential facts of their stories are true and current. First, let's take a look at Chris, now in his late 20s. Chris was the out-of-wedlock child of a teenage mother.

> *From the outset, Chris was clearly hyperactive. In addition to his unstoppable energy, Chris, a handsome boy, was very talkative and curious. When he entered school he showed no patience for the passive activities of reading and writing. Luckily for Chris, his family did not turn Chris's dislike of school into a huge battle.*
>
> *Chris's mother and stepfather owned and managed a small family business. After school each day Chris walked to his parents' store. He was gradually put to work in the store and thus learned to function in the business world as naturally as he had learned to talk.*
>
> *Chris loved automobiles and talked of little else. At 16 he was hired by an automobile agency. At 18 Chris became the youngest car salesman ever at the dealership. His ready smile, his energy, and his sociability carried him far. By the age of 30, this ADD high school graduate owned his own home, drove an expensive company car, and earned over $50,000 per year. He was brimming with enthusiasm and self-confidence.*

John was the son of a highly regarded businessman. He grew up in the suburbs of Washington, D.C., attending one of the competitive, upper-middle-class suburban high schools from which many students go on to top colleges and universities. John, to the embarrassment of his parents, was a poor student. Although bright, he showed no motivation in high school.

Prompted by depression, frustration, and chronic conflicts with his parents, John drifted into frequent marijuana use and fairly heavy drinking in his late adolescence. He entered the local community college, but his lethargy and low motivation continued. Meanwhile he developed an interest in computers and electronics. He dropped out of community college to seek training in a local computer school to become a computer technician.

You might ask yourself at this point, "How is this a success story?" John's story begins differently from Chris's largely because of the conflict he had with his parents. In John's case there was a tremendous gap between natural inclinations and parental expectations.

After John completed his 9-month course in computer programming, he found an entry level job as a computer technician. Several years later he married. With the support of a non-ADD wife and with the responsibilities of marriage, John's attitude toward education began to change. He slowly began to take college courses at night. This time, with a focus and with motivation, he set his sights on a degree in computer science.

By his mid-30s, John had earned his computer science degree and had received several promotions at work. In his early 40s he earned a master's degree in business administration.

By his mid-40s, John held a very responsible position, in the computer science industry.

What factors had led to John's eventual success?

- He had wisely decided to pursue a career path that greatly interested him and for which he showed a natural talent.

- He was helped tremendously by the support and structure provided by his non-ADD spouse, who believed in him and encouraged him to pursue his interests.

- He was able to motivate and discipline himself to continue his education because he selected courses of study that had a direct and practical relationship to his work.

- And he persisted. John's education, which another person might have completed by age 25, was not completed until age 45.

It is critical that adults with ADD not measure themselves by the yardstick of "normality." As we saw with John, many adults who become successful despite ADD do so later than their peers and via a more nontraditional path.

> *Mark sought help for his ADD in his early 30s, when he feared losing his job as an accountant. He was the son of a successful accountant and had chosen that career, after failing to earn a degree in engineering. Although he was highly intelligent, curious, and had a lively imagination, Mark had never shown much discipline or motivation to succeed in school.*
>
> *Although Mark was intelligent and likable, his habitual late arrival and indifferent work habits finally prompted his supervisor to give him a stern warning. Mark discussed his career problems with a friend, who suggested that his lifelong problems with self-discipline and motivation might be related to ADD. Mark sought an evaluation, and his friend's suspicions were quickly confirmed. He embarked on a treatment program that included both medication and career-oriented counseling.*

(story continued . . .)

Mark's low motivation at work and at school were in great contrast to his intense interest in a wide range of hobbies. Now he began to explore, with his counselor, ways that his work life could become more fun. Mark loved computers and was gregarious, with a gift for verbal expression. It had simply never occurred to him that these interests and abilities might be applied to his career in accounting.

He began to explore with his supervisor the possibility of transferring to a job in the firm that would take advantage of his computer expertise and his natural gift for teaching and explaining. The more convincingly he demonstrated his new-found motivation at work, the more willing his supervisor became to support him in new career directions.

Two years after Mark's initial diagnosis of ADD, he was happily ensconced in a new position with his firm, training coworkers to use new software systems. He was excited about his work, which was a good match for his interests and abilities, and felt positive about his future in the firm.

7 POSITIVE SIDE

What were the factors that led to Mark's career success?

- His high native ability.
- Positive ADD traits—curiosity, inventiveness, high energy level, and a gregarious, outgoing nature.
- He responded well to treatment for his ADD.
- He was able to carve out a niche that was a very good match for his interests and abilities.

Karen's success was entirely self-made. She sought an evaluation in her late 50s after reading articles on ADD. The story she told was of almost heroic proportions.

Karen was raised in a dysfunctional home. Her parents divorced when she was young. Her mother, not highly educated herself, had little time or energy to devote to her daughter. This timid, underweight little girl was sent to classes for underachievers, where she languished for years.

She was almost illiterate when she graduated from high school, but somewhere inside this young woman there developed a steely determination to change her life. She set about to teach herself to read—and was successful in her efforts! Despite a low-paying job and a failing marriage, she decided to go to college.

Karen's one stroke of luck was to land a job as a secretary for a government agency that paid her tuition as a fringe benefit. Her self-discipline and determination were evident on the job, and she was gradually promoted to higher and higher positions.

When Karen finally sought an ADD evaluation, in her late 50s, she reported that she had successfully raised her two children, had finally earned her college degree, was an active union representative, and had been taking courses in law school for the past several years. Her hope was that with the benefit of treatment for her difficulties in concentration she could take a leave of absence from her job, go to school full-time, and succeed in her goal of becoming a labor lawyer! All this from a woman who was nearly illiterate and almost without a family when she graduated from high school.

The keys to Karen's success are more difficult to pinpoint, but they certainly include:

- Determination
- Perseverance

- Encouragement from professors
- Opportunity (through a tuition reimbursement program at work)

Karen's story is inspiring as an example of how strong motivation can overcome enormous odds.

As you can see from these stories, success in life with ADD can be reached through a variety of channels. All these people reached success by finding a type of work for which they were well suited and in which they were highly interested. Furthermore, in spite of the academic difficulties they each experienced, related to their ADD, they all possessed some positive ADD characteristics as well, which led to their success. They learned how to make ADD work for them rather than against them!

7 POSITIVE SIDE

In this chapter we look at ADD success traits on the job, by examining the success factors of ADD author Thom Hartmann and the research conducted by Paul Gerber on highly successful adults with learning disabilities.

Success Strategies in the Workplace

What You Need to Become an "ADD Success Story"

Paul Gerber, a social scientist, has studied highly successful adults with learning disabilities to see what they held in common.[1] Although, learning disabilities and ADD are not synonymous, you can learn a great deal about what you may need in your own professional life by studying Dr. Gerber's findings. He discovered common internal traits as well as shared circumstances, which seemed to support the extraordinary success of these individuals.

Gerber's Internal Success Factors

First, let's take a look at the internal traits that Dr. Gerber found in successful adults with learning disabilities.

1. Strong Motivation

All of the highly successful adults with learning disabilities who were studied by Dr. Gerber reported that they were highly motivated to achieve success in their careers and were willing to put in the required effort.

2. Determination

None of the highly successful adults interviewed by Dr. Gerber were easily deterred from their goals or easily discouraged in the face of temporary setbacks.

3. Strong Need to Control One's Life and Future

Dr. Gerber's subjects were all people who had set goals for themselves and who very much wanted to be in charge of their efforts to achieve those goals. In other words, they were highly self-determined, self-directed individuals.

4. Capacity to See One's Disability in a Positive Light

Successful learning disabled individuals have learned to "reframe" their disabilities to see them in a positive light. A similar "reframing" of ADD is reflected in the humorous title of Kate Kelly and Peggy Ramundo's book about ADD in adults: *You Mean I'm Not Lazy, Stupid or Crazy?!*[2]

5. A Planned, Goal-Oriented Approach

All of the successful adults with LD worked hard at charting a course for their futures and outlining the steps they needed to take. They reached their success through *intention*, not by chance.

6. Ability to Seek Help When Needed Without Becoming Dependent

Successful adults with LD developed a realistic picture of their strengths and weaknesses, and were comfortable in seeking assistance and guidance when needed. At the same time, they remained focused, goal-oriented, and independent.

Internal Success Factors from an ADD Perspective

The good news is that the first three traits are often found in adults with ADD.

1. **Strong motivation:** Given a subject of high interest, adults with ADD can seem unstoppable!

2. **Determination:** Call it stubborn, call it determined, the strong-willed nature of many with ADD can lead to tremendous accomplishment if directed in a positive way.

3. **Strong need to control one's life and future:** Described negatively, this might be expressed as accepting supervision poorly! The adult with ADD needs to translate his not liking to be told what to do into charting his own course.

Considered together, this trio of determination, motivation, and independence have played major roles in the success stories of adults with ADD.

4. **Capacity to see ADD in a positive light:** This is an essential corner to turn, and can be a difficult one for those who have received more criticism than support in their lives. Often counseling can help you change your self-concept from "defective" to "different"—with a recognition of all the positive traits included in that difference.

5. **A planned, goal-oriented approach:** The ability to maintain a planned, goal-oriented approach is the internal factor that requires the most work and effort for adults with ADD to develop. Why? The problem for adults with ADD often comes when it is time to harness all their energy, determination, and independence by charting a course and sticking to it. They must learn to be actors rather than reactors.

Ned Hallowell writes in *Answers to Distraction*[3] that many ADD adults resist structure, feeling it will hamper their creativity and enjoyment. Dr. Hallowell explains, however, that the right kind of structure actually enhances and promotes creativity. He emphasizes how important it is for ADD adults to be in charge of the structure rather than feel that it is imposed on them (remember the need that ADD adults have to be in charge of their own destiny!).

6. **Ability to seek help when needed without becoming dependent**—Seeking help may be difficult for some adults with ADD. Frank Sinatra's "My Way" could be their theme song. Although independence can be a very positive trait, it can become bullheadedness if taken too far. An "I don't take advice from anyone" attitude can lead to enormous problems. If you experience great discomfort when being supervised by others or when seeking advice from others, it may be extremely important for you to work on this issue in psychotherapy; you should also take extra care to work under a compatible supervisor.

External Success Factors

Now let's take a look at the external factors that supported the success of the adults with learning disabilities whom Paul Gerber studied. These people found success either through sheer good fortune or through personal insight and initiative. By reading this book, you yourself have the tremendous advantage of learning from the experience of others. What did all these people have in common in their work environment?

1. A Mentor

Mentorship can take different forms. Mentors enjoy the role of passing on the wisdom and experience they have gained over many years in their field, and younger employees flourish under the supportive tutelage of their mentors and provide increasingly valuable support to their mentors as they grow professionally.

It can be a long-standing relationship or a series of mentors as a younger worker moves from one rung of the career ladder to the next. One highly successful young woman reported that the most important trait she sought in a supervisor was the ability to be a mentor. She actively sought supervisors whose experience was greater and whose knowledge would help her advance in her career.

Some adults with ADD actively avoid placing themselves in the position of having mentors. Unlike the self-directed, determined young woman who readily recognized the value of a mentor, they fear that they are giving up autonomy by seeking advice. It's important to keep in mind that the guidance of a mentor is not something imposed on you; rather, it comes from a relationship that you initiate and from which you directly benefit.

2. Positive, Supportive Coworkers

When he interviewed successful people with learning disabilities, Paul Gerber found that they worked in a friendly, supportive environment. Such an environment is just as important for people with ADD (more about this in Chapter 9). As is true of the best academic environment, the best workplace is one in which you feel supported and encouraged. Surrounded by emotional support, you are more relaxed, less likely to make ADD-related errors, and more able to take risks in order to grow professionally.

The power of a positive work environment is strongly reflected in Amy's story.

> *Amy had been diagnosed with ADD and learning disabilities as a child. Despite a high IQ, she had never done well in school, partly because she resisted all forms of treatment and intervention.*

> *(story continued . . .)*
>
> *After graduating from high school, Amy drifted from one dead-end job to another until she was hired, entirely by chance, by a couple who ran a small family business. The personal chemistry between Amy and her employers was very positive. They recognized her intelligence, and she thrived in the first environment where she felt truly appreciated. Amy became a model employee—highly reliable and enthusiastic. As she learned more and more about the business, she began to believe, for the first time, that she was smart, something her parents and teachers had always told her.*
>
> *Even better, Amy's confidence helped her grow in other ways. She became friendly with the owner's son, a college student her own age. Hanging around college students for the first time in her life, she began to think of greater possibilities in her future. To her own amazement, a few years after her disastrous high school experience she was thinking of taking college courses and realized that her future held a wide range of choices.*

Amy's history is a clear example of the importance of finding positive, supportive people to work among. The couple for whom she worked served as mentors (and even quasi-parents) for her as she struggled to develop the self-esteem that had been so eroded during her school years. In the past, Amy had painfully learned that failure leads to failure; she was now in the process of learning that success breeds success!

3. New Work Experiences to Enhance Skills

Paul Gerber's study found that successful learning disabled adults found work experiences that allowed them to grow and develop. For adults with ADD, however, this aspect of a job is critical. In order to overcome difficulties with concentration, follow-through, and motivation, it is essential that individuals with ADD find work that continues to interest them, work that allows variety and at least a moderate degree of challenge. Boredom and repetition are the dreaded components of any job for an adult with ADD.

> *John had experienced success in his work life despite ADD, which was only identified in his late 50s when his son, age 25, was diagnosed. Financial success had never been a primary goal for John. Rather, he valued freedom, variety, creativity, and change. His resume was remarkably varied. At the time of his diagnosis he was living on a sailboat with his second wife and working as a building contractor.*
>
> *I met John when he was doing remodeling work for me. A voluble man, he once explained to me that whenever he became truly bored with his current job, he began making mistakes.*
>
> *John was working in my kitchen, constructing a table, at the time of this particular conversation. A few minutes later, I heard a loud curse. I quickly returned to the kitchen, and found him, electric saw in hand, gazing with consternation at a gash he had cut in the nearly finished tabletop. He turned to me and said, "This is one of those moments that tells me it's time to move on!" And, indeed, he did just that. When I heard from him a few months later, he had quit the home remodeling business and had started a new business with his wife.*

The small line of wood putty, barely discernible on the kitchen table, has always reminded me that boredom and repetition lead to problems for many adults with ADD. Whether you move on to an entirely new venture, or find new and interesting activities within your current field, it is essential for people with ADD to have new work experiences to grow, develop, and maintain interest.

4. A Work Environment Where Help Is Available When Needed

Readily available help is, of course, a critical part of any supportive work environment and an essential feature of an ADD-friendly workplace. I would add a qualification: that the help be available informally and on an as-needed basis. Because ADD adults so typically have difficulty with time management, planning, and organization, it is much more helpful for them to work in an environment where they can get an on-the-spot answer to a question than in one where the supervisor says, "Write down your questions, and we'll talk about them in our supervisory session at the end of the week." People with ADD, whether in an academic or a work environment, typically find that when help is provided in a procedural, bureaucratic fashion, it has limited effectiveness and is used infrequently.

5. A Good Fit between Skills and Job Requirements

Because people with learning disabilities and ADD typically have strengths and weaknesses in the area of job skills, it is particularly important that the primary demands of their job be those that are related to their strengths and that tasks related to their weaknesses constitute a minor part of their job. While this combination would be beneficial to anyone, it is much more critical for those with ADD because the difference between their skills and weaknesses is great. As many with ADD have painfully learned, you can feel and appear incompetent if you are placed in a work (or academic) situation that calls on you to function in your areas of greatest weakness.

The Essential ADD Success Factor

To the five aforementioned external factors important to job success, I would add a critical sixth element for adults with ADD: a good fit between one's **interests** and the requirements of one's job.

The word interests is written in bold because this cannot be emphasized enough! Adults with ADD who have a high degree of interest in their work generally find that their ADD problems (such as careless errors, forgetfulness, distractibility, poor follow-through) are minimized while their ADD positive traits (ability to hyper-focus for long periods of time, high energy level, determination) are stimulated.

Hartmann's Success Factors

Thom Hartmann, in his book *Focus Your Energy*,[4] talks about three other success traits he has found among successful ADD entrepreneurs:

- Individualism
- Creativity
- Need for high stimulation

Their individualism led them to seek entrepreneurial activities rather than remain within a bureaucratic structure. Their creativity led them to new ideas, including the envisioning of new market niches. Finally, their need for high stimulation led them to move on to new tasks, challenges, and ventures. Hartmann emphasizes that failure for such talented ADD individuals tended to occur when they had to shift from their high-energy–high-creativity mode to a more predictable and mundane managerial mode as their enterprise developed and matured. To accommodate to this almost inevitable cycle, Hartmann suggests that such ADD adults plan in advance to turn over management of their enterprise to others so that they can move on to do what they love best—engage in the next creative adventure! (For more information about success traits in entrepreneurs with ADD, see the books by Thom Hartmann cited in the Reference section at the end of this book.)

Conclusion

Researchers have spent most of their time emphasizing the negative aspects of the neurochemical disorder called ADD. On the other hand, Paul Gerber's research stresses that it is quite possible to attain professional success despite learning disabilities (which are in many ways parallel to ADD). Thom Hartmann goes even further: He challenges the notion that ADD is a disorder at all. He turns the negative point of view on its head and looks at the potential good that can result from the supposedly negative symptoms of ADD. Both authors present a hopeful message. By studying the traits shared by successful people with ADD, you can learn ways to both take charge of your ADD-related problems and take advantage of the positive aspects of ADD.

8 SUCCESS STRATEGIES

An ADD-Friendly Work Environment

What is an ADD-Friendly Work Environment?

The key to success begins with understanding yourself and your needs. Adults with ADD have a variety of needs. A work environment in which most of these needs are met can be described as "ADD friendly." Knowing your own needs is critical to your finding or creating an ADD-friendly environment.

An ADD-friendly work environment is one that enhances your ability to function well as an adult with ADD. A number of factors—both physical and interpersonal—make a workplace ADD-friendly. Your relationship with your boss or immediate supervisor is certainly one of the most important factors—important enough to merit a separate chapter in this book (see Chapter 10).

There are ADD-friendly job factors that apply to most adults with ADD, but there are undoubtedly other factors critical for you that are not mentioned here. It cannot be repeated enough that (1) there are wide differences among adults with ADD and that (2) you, as an adult with ADD, need to take responsibility for yourself, your choices, and for advocating for your needs on the job.

Low Stress

S tress is extremely ADD-unfriendly. Adults with ADD are more susceptible to the effects of stress than are their non-ADD colleagues.[1] High stress increases ADD symptoms. Increased severity of ADD symptoms are typically one of the first signs of stress. You may think that you are calm during a particularly stressful period at work, but then suddenly you realize that you are forgetting more things, are less organized, and are letting things slip through the cracks. During periods when your ADD seems worse, the first culprit to look for is stress.

How is stress created? Although the same things are not stressors for all people, the following are commonly considered to be stressors on the job:

Stress Factors on the Job
Long hours at work
A long commute in heavy traffic
Fear of being fired
Fear for the company's future
New management
Crisis-style management
High criticism and low praise from a supervisor
Unrealistic demands for high productivity
Frequent deadlines
Financial concerns
Unclear duties and responsibilities
Conflictual relationships with coworkers
Promotion that emphasizes areas of weakness

We are only focusing here on workplace stressors, but stressors in your personal life can also have a negative impact on your ADD symptoms at work. These should be monitored and managed as well.

**Low stress
=
ADD friendly**

Stimulation

S tress should not be confused with stimulation. Stress refers to things that are distressing, whereas a stimulating job challenges you, piques your interest, gets your juices flowing. Ideal levels of stimulation can reduce ADD symptoms! Each person has his or her own level of optimal stimulation. It is important that you learn what your optimal level of stimulation is and that you learn ways to create and maintain that optimal level.

When you are working at your optimal level of stimulation, you are most likely to function in a focused, creative, and tremendously effective fashion. However, stimulation is a double-edged sword. While optimal stimulation can reduce ADD symptoms and maximize effectiveness, overstimulation can be stress and can increase your ADD symptoms.

How would you rate the stimulation level of your current job? In most jobs the stimulation level varies. Your goal should be to find or create a job that has the right level of stimulation most of the time. It may help to review all of your previous jobs and to rate each of them in terms of stimulation. Here are some things that might be helpful to think about as you consider the stimulation level of your current job:

- Your level of interest in the job
- Opportunity for creativity

- Degree of challenge presented by your job

- Opportunity to learn new skills

- Degree of interaction with others

- Opportunity for travel

- Pace of work

- Degree of freedom to pursue your own interests

UNDERSTIMULATION
Repetitive, Routine, Boring

OPTIMAL STIMULATION
Challenging, Interesting, Engaging

OVERSTIMULATION
Overwhelming, Exhausting, Frenzied

Stimulation and Personality Type

What is stimulating varies from person to person, according to interests and personality type (see Chapter 6, ADD and Personality Type at Work).[2,3] In this section certain aspects of personality are discussed, as defined by the Myers-Briggs Type Indicator.

If you are not sure of your personality type, you may find it helpful to take the Myers-Briggs Type Indicator so that you can take your type into account as you think about how to create your optimal stimulation zone at work.

Extroversion–Introversion

Extroverts (E's) need people interaction to function optimally. E's who are isolated run the risk of slumping into the "understimulation zone," where they may experience boredom and restlessness and are prone to underfunctioning. Introverts (I's), by contrast, should guard against too much interpersonal interaction that may push them into the "over-stimulation zone," where ADD symptoms worsen.

Sensing–Intuition

Sensors (S's) function best when they are busy accomplishing practical things—making, fixing, building, curing, or solving practical problems. S's often find it very satisfying to do things with their hands. An S will not be stimulated by an "all talk and no action" environment. Intuitives (N's), on the other hand, are most stimulated by that very environment. N's love the world of ideas, the world of the possible rather than the actual. N's are stimulated in the best way when they are imagining, writing, creating, and thinking.

Thinking–Feeling

Thinkers (T's) love to analyze in a detached, problem-solving fashion. A group of T's may feel wonderfully stimulated as they work to understand why a machine is malfunctioning or how a certain economic formula may be applied. This same group of T's, however, may feel terribly stressed when the problem that needs solving involves people and feelings. The people-oriented problems that are typically stressful to T's are life's blood to Feelers (F's), who are most stimulated by working with people, by empathizing, helping, and doing something "meaningful." F's would feel detached and understimulated if they did work that involved things instead of people.

Judging–Perceiving

Judgers (J's) thrive on structure and will try to create it if it isn't provided in the work environment. J's tend to find an unpredictable work environment highly stressful and distracting, whereas organization and structure help them find their zone of optimal stimulation. Perceivers (P's) are in their optimal zone when they have the freedom to be spontaneous and flexible. In a highly structured, rigid work environment, a P will feel either bored (high structure, slow pace) or stressed (high structure, fast pace).

ADD Traits and Optimal Stimulation

In addition to personality factors, there are a number of ADD traits that vary from one ADD adult to another and that strongly influence the degree and types of stimulation desirable at work.

Intolerance of Routine

Many adults with ADD have little tolerance for routine. Their needs for change and challenge may translate into changing jobs with some frequency. These individuals love the challenge and creativity involved in developing a program or product, but they become bored or frustrated with the day-to-day operations of maintaining what they have created. Thom Hartmann talks about this phenomenon among entrepreneurs with ADD and strongly counsels them to plan on turning over the day-to-day operations of their enterprises to a managerial type.[4]

Challenge of Problem-Solving

Some adults with ADD recognize a pattern of restlessness and need for change in themselves and actively seek work that allows opportunity for job change. One adult with ADD, for example, is employed in a think tank in Washington, D.C. He reports that this job is ideal for him because every few weeks or months he is working on a new project with different people and is traveling to different places. His rapid flow of creative ideas resulting from his ADD is a strong asset for him in this work situation. Another gifted adult with ADD has developed a career making educational documentaries for television. Again, his need for change and stimulation and his flow of creative ideas make him ideally suited to this type of work (although he has learned to leave the administrative details to others!).

Physical Stimulation

Some adults with ADD find that they need the stimulation provided by action, movement, and physical change. These are the "don't fence me in" types who typically report that they could never sit behind a desk all day. Rather than the intellectual stimulation required by some, these ADD adults like geographical change and physical movement.

> One man with ADD developed his own private demolition company. He loved the risk, the movement, the rough-and-tumble interaction with the men who worked under him. Another action-oriented ADD adult went into the car auction business. Crisscrossing several states in his region of the country, he bought cars at auction and resold them to local dealers. He loved the irregular schedule, the easy social interaction with other men at the auction, and the challenge of recognizing the worth of a car and making a shrewd bargain.

> Yet another man with ADD held a job as the head of a construction crew employed by a large company with franchised outlets around the country. The crew's task was to completely remodel shopping center space to the specifications of the company within a period of 3 to 5 days. This ADD adult liked the variety and challenge inherent in designing and building to suit a particular space and franchisee. Like other restless, hyperactive ADD men, he liked alternating between the intensity of the work and the several days of slack time between work periods.

Social Stimulation

Social stimulation is essential for some adults with ADD. Sales, lobbying, politics, entertainment, and public relations all hold an appeal for ADD adults who have a strong need for social stimulation. Of course, there are adults with ADD who are drawn to combinations of these sources of stimulation. One young woman, for example, finally chose to leave the academic environment, which she had found too sedentary and frustrating, to enter the world of haute cuisine. There she found a combination of physical activity, social interaction, opportunity for creativity, and constant new challenges.

Thinking about the types of stimulation described in the preceding several paragraphs in light of your particular ADD tendencies and personality traits may help you gain a better understanding of the types of stimulation that are best for you.

> *One ADD young man had an incredible stroke of luck when his family arranged for him to become a page on Capitol Hill in Washington, D.C., during his high school years. Because he was extremely restless and had little interest in academics, he would probably have done poorly in a typical high school environment. On Capitol Hill, however, the pages attend high school only a few hours each morning and then spend the remainder of their day talking, interacting, and running errands for busy senators and representatives. It was a perfect environment for him. Rather than attending college, he remained on Capitol Hill, where he was widely known and admired, and worked his way into higher levels of employment on the force of his energy, personality, and experience.*

Freedom from Distractions

Another important factor in the ideal ADD-friendly work environment is the intensity and frequency of distractions. People with ADD struggle with problems of distraction under the best of circumstances. It's important to look for a work environment that is as nondistracting as possible. In the modular office environment so common today, freedom from the following distractors is not easy to achieve:

- Conversations of coworkers
- People traffic
- Phone calls
- Interruptions by coworkers, messengers, visitors
- General noise pollution from the operation of office equipment

Seek a Quiet Work Space

The ideal setting for an adult with ADD is, of course, a private office. For most workers, however, this is not a feasible option. If you work in a modular environment, ask for a cubicle out of the line of traffic. Seek a cubicle that is not near the photocopying machine, the water fountain, the boss's office, or along the main corridor down which everyone walks. If you lack even the benefit of a modular office space, you can request portable screens to surround your desk on three sides to cut down on both visual and auditory distractions.

Noise pollution can be diminished through the use of headphones or a small white noise machine near your desk. Visual distraction can be minimized by placing your desk chair so that you face away from the opening to your cubicle. Other important visual distractors, however, may be found within your own cubicle! Even non-ADD adults tend to work more efficiently when they work in a neat, orderly work space with a clean desktop.

Schedule Interruptions

The interruption of phone calls can be minimized by taking all your calls as voice mail. In that way you can set aside blocks of time to listen to your voice mail and return calls at your own convenience, instead of allowing random incoming calls to interrupt your work and destroy your concentration. One man with ADD had to make an additional accommodation for a boss who needed to be able to contact him immediately rather than resort to voice mail: He carried a beeper that signaled him that his boss had called so that he could return the call immediately.

Time-Shift Your Work Hours

Meetings and casual interruptions are essential to manage if you are to function efficiently in the workplace as an adult with ADD. One way to enhance work efficiency is to arrive early or stay late, so that you have a block of time each day with few, if any, interruptions. If you are working on an important project, ask permission to be absent from nonessential meetings so that your train of thought isn't broken. It is helpful to develop an automatic, diplomatic way to let people who drop by your office for a quick question or comment know you are busy. Better yet, suggest that they send you E-mail or a memo!

Minimal Paperwork

It is no surprise that paperwork tends to be the bane of the workplace for adults with ADD. Paperwork entails all the functions that are difficult and frustrating for people with attentional problems, namely, attending to detail, organizing thoughts, meeting deadlines, and fighting boredom.

One man with ADD held a rather high-level government position in which he enjoyed the services of an administrative assistant. Through a departmental reorganization he lost his assistant. Shortly thereafter his performance ratings began to decline. The mountains of paperwork, for which the government is well known, became overwhelming. Although he could perform the more complex interpersonal and intellectual aspects

> *(story continued)*
> *of his work, he found himself unable to keep up with paper-work demands. His once promising career deteriorated into an unsatisfying job for which he was ill suited.*

Other adults with ADD have reported similar, though less dramatic, stories. Keeping track of travel expenses and time sheets is often a chronic point of tension for adults with ADD.

> *One young man with ADD was employed as a social worker in a large social service agency. His job was to interview many people each day to determine their eligibility for various social services. Each client was required to provide a rather large number of documents. The social worker was expected to keep track of each case, to complete all paperwork, and to keep a record of documents that were yet to be provided by each client. After several months on the job he was hopelessly behind. A mountain of charts lay in complete disarray on his desk. After repeated warnings, he was finally asked to leave his position owing to his inability to keep up with the paperwork. Fortunately, this young man sought treatment for his ADD. In the course of his therapy, he formulated a plan to seek a job in which he could use his social work training but that had minimal paperwork requirements. He found such work in a psychiatric hospital, where his duties were to interact with patients and staff, lead group meetings, give oral reports on the status of each patient, and write a brief note in each patient's chart at the end of his daily shift. By finding an ADD-friendly position, he changed from an employee with an unsatisfactory work record to a highly regarded, dedicated staff member.*

Needless to say, in seeking an ADD-friendly job, it is important to look for one in which paperwork is simplified, streamlined, and deemphasized—or, best of all, one in which you can seek the assistance of someone else to keep up with the flow of paperwork!

Short-Term Projects

An important feature of ADD-friendly work is involvement with projects of limited duration. Complicated long-term projects can result in diminished interest over time, procrastination, reduced motivation, poor planning, faulty follow-through, and strained organizational skills. Adults with ADD are often much better suited for more immediate tasks.

> *One woman with ADD had a job that involved responding immediately to incoming telephone calls. Each caller had specific questions that had to be researched and responded to on the spot. There was no opportunity for procrastination, no requirement to respond to several calls at once, and no possibility of becoming forgetful or disorganized. The woman described this as the perfect job for her ADD. She always had something immediate and different to stimulate her, and there was no leftover paperwork at the end of the day.*

Help with Long-Term Projects

Long-term projects that require planning and organizational skills are often the downfall of adults with ADD. If you are in a job with a strong emphasis on such projects, your best approach is to emphasize teamwork so that individuals better suited to the planning and monitoring of the project can take major responsibility for those aspects, leaving you freer to focus on problem solving (often an ADD strength) or on short, clearly defined aspects of the long-term project.

An ADD-friendly job that entails long-term projects will provide the following:

Clearly defined short-term tasks.

Regular (weekly, perhaps even daily) feedback from a supervisor

Teamwork with someone more skilled in long-term planning

"Big Picture" Emphasis

The ideal ADD-friendly job is one in which the "big picture" skills of the adult with ADD are emphasized and the details are left to a more focused, detail-oriented non-ADD individual. Hard to manage details often include:

Scheduling

Paperwork requirements

Multistep bureaucratic procedures

Keeping track of addresses and phone numbers

Filing

Limited Supervisory Responsibility

Being promoted to a position that requires the supervision and management of others can be the downfall of an adult with ADD since such a position requires one to monitor and guide others, attend to details, and assume multiple, sometimes competing, responsibilities. These tasks tend to be difficult for adults with ADD who have difficulty with self-monitoring and in attending to the details of their own work. When the responsibility for others is added, they may become overwhelmed and disorganized.

Promotions Can Be a Downfall

The promotion, the raise, the prestige are often temptations too strong to resist. ADD adults who have worked hard to become expert in their field often find that when they are promoted to management, they shift from peak functioning to faltering. They have moved into a position that calls on their weaknesses rather than their strengths.

Be Realistic

There are certainly ADD people whose symptoms are mild or whose compensatory skills are excellent who can do an adequate or even good job as a manager. If you decide to accept such a position, though, it is important that you recognize the potential pitfalls. If you have made your best efforts and find the job still isn't right for you, don't try to hang in there no matter what. Recognize the problem for what it is, namely, a job that emphasizes your areas of weakness, and head for a more ADD-friendly position.

Breaks from Extended Concentration

Long conferences and half-day or all-day meetings are extremely tiring and stressful for those with ADD. They typically surpass the concentration span of non-ADD adults. An "ADD-friendly" job rarely requires the individual to focus and concentrate for such long periods without opportunity for breaks. If you are in a job where such meetings are inevitable, arrange to take brief breaks independently if enough breaks are not scheduled during the meeting. In addition some adults with ADD find that their attention span is extended if they take notes during the meeting.

Opportunity for Movement

A chance to move about frequently during the workday is very important for restless or hyperactive adults. Ideally such movement is a natural part of the job. Some adults who are on the hyperactive end of the spectrum specifically look for jobs in which they are on their feet and moving about most of the day.

Physical Environment

An ADD-friendly physical environment has good lighting, clean air, and a comfortable temperature; is reasonably quiet, spacious, and orderly; and includes a comfortable desk and chair. People with ADD are sometimes hypersensitive to certain aspects of their physical environment, aspects that may be only minor irritants to others. If this is true for you, there is no need to feel defensive or apologetic; often there is a neurological basis for this type of hypersensitivity. Hypersensitive children, for example, may be extremely irritated by wool or scratchy material and even by labels and seams in their clothing. Such hypersensitivity may be due to problems with what is called sensory integration.

You may find that you are bothered by loud sounds or by sounds at certain pitches. Some people with ADD are extra sensitive to the flickering of fluorescent lighting. Irritants in the physical work environment all take their toll, increasing fatigue, distractibility, and other ADD symptoms. Don't condemn yourself as being too picky if you find that you are more sensitive than your coworkers to environmental irritants; you're not being picky, you're being "ADD-smart."

High Interest

It almost goes without saying that an ADD-friendly job is one that holds your interest. In fact, high interest and motivation are two of the most powerful forces to use in your battle against ADD problems. There is no magic formula for determining which job will be of high interest to a specific individual, but reading this book may help you in making your choice.

Conclusion

To sum it all up, there are many important factors that in combination create an ADD-friendly work environment.

A Quick Checklist of ADD-Friendly Job Characteristics

1. Low stress
2. Optimal stimulation
3. Nondistracting workspace
4. Minimal paperwork
5. Short-term projects
6. Assistance with long-term projects
7. Emphasis on the "big picture"—not on details
8. Limited supervisory duties
9. Opportunity for movement / breaks from demand for concentration
10. Comfortable physical environment
11. High interest activity

No workplace environment is perfect. It is ureasonable to ask for perfection, but you should take your reactions seriously. Think about yourself and your reactions to the workplace factors listed in this chapter. Then compare the most important factors to your current workplace environment. Can you think of creative ways to reduce and minimize problems? Perhaps this chapter will give you ideas of ways to improve your current job and of things to look for in your next job.

If you have an opportunity to make a transfer within your company or if you are in the process of looking for a new job, this chapter can offer a few guidelines for seeking a good fit between you and your new supervisor.

The Ideal Boss

Why Fantasize About an Ideal Boss?

"Why think about an ideal boss if I'm stuck with the one I have?" At several points in this book parallels have been drawn between workplace issues for adults with ADD and school issues for children with ADD. Here is another important parallel: Just as children often have little or no choice of teacher, so too do adults have little latitude in choosing a supervisor. Nevertheless, it is an important issue to consider for several reasons.

First, you won't always be working under your current supervisor. You may transfer or leave your job, and your supervisor may do likewise. Second, believe it or not, some supervisors are motivated to become better supervisors! Your current supervisor has probably had no training in how best to work with an adult with ADD. Owing to lack of information, he or she may have developed approaches that are uncomfortable or ineffective for you. If you have a reasonably positive relationship with your supervisor, you may be able to communicate some of the information contained in this chapter to him or her and develop a dialogue that leads to a more productive relationship.

Third, when you do have a choice—that is, when you are job hunting, either within your current organization or somewhere else—you will know which qualities to look for.

Who Is the Ideal Supervisor for an Adult with ADD?

A better question to ask is "What's *my* ideal supervisor like?" Not all people with ADD are alike. Some need a high degree of structure and predictability in a supervisor; others flourish under a more laissez-faire attitude. Some people with ADD are hypersensitive to stress and need a calm, predictable work environment; others crave stimulation and variety and would find such an environment boring. Nevertheless, there are certain characteristics to be found among great bosses and others that define "bosses from hell."

ADD Tales from the Workplace

A Boss from Hell

John was a bright computer whiz who was highly regarded in a rapidly growing high-tech company. Because of his expertise in software development and his engaging manner, he was targeted for a promotion that involved public relations and new product development.

> *John's problems began shortly after starting work in his new position. Unfortunately, his new boss was somewhat insecure and had relatively little supervisory experience. He misinterpreted John's easygoing style as laziness, his ADD forgetfulness as irresponsibility, his need to shift from one task to another in order to maintain interest and motivation as disorganization, and his ideas and suggestions for change as a direct challenge to his authority as a supervisor.*

10 IDEAL BOSS

(story continued)

 John's performance deteriorated under the tension, lack of support, and frequent criticisms from his boss. The more depressed and discouraged he became, the less he was able to function. His boss's style was to focus on his supervisees' inadequacies and to rarely, if ever, emphasize things that were going well.

 As his morale sank to dangerous levels, John sought ADD-oriented career counseling. He requested that his psychologist write a letter clearly outlining the types of assistance and accommodations he needed at work.

 Unfortunately, this supervisor didn't "believe" in ADD and felt angry that he was required under the Americans with Disabilities Act to provide accommodations. His approach was to adhere to the letter but not the spirit of the recommendations.

 John wasn't fired, but his supervisor clearly intended to make him want to resign. After several months of unbearable tension between them, John realized that it was futile to continue to attempt to gain his boss's support and confidence.

  What were the characteristics of this supervisor that made him an "ADD boss from hell"? John's supervisor:

- Was nonsupportive
- Was inflexible
- Overfocused on details
- Misinterpreted ADD symptoms
- Didn't recognize the strengths his supervisee brought to the job
- Had a strong need for control
- Felt threatened by his supervisee's questions and requests

- Didn't "believe in" ADD
- Resented being asked to make accommodations for ADD symptoms
- Emphasized negative traits

Fear of enduring an experience like John's is what makes many adults with ADD reluctant to disclose their disorder. Such reactions are not universal, though. Furthermore, there are many things you can do without formally disclosing your ADD diagnosis to improve your work environment. Now let's take a look at a supervisory relationship that worked beautifully.

An Ideal ADD Supervisor

Ann was a middle-aged woman who returned to full-time work after raising her children. Although she was a college graduate, she had always had difficulty in school, without knowing why, and had found school very stressful. Only years later, after the evaluation of a son who was diagnosed with ADD and learning problems, did Ann come to understand that she had struggled with ADD without benefit of diagnosis or treatment.

Ann decided to seek testing and treatment to smooth her reentry into the workplace environment.

Ann was hired as an administrative assistant to one of the deans at a local university. She was selected because of her obvious intelligence, excellent verbal skills, and warm, caring manner. The dean, who was looking for someone who would serve as a "welcoming committee" for the many people who sought contact with her in person and on the phone, immediately recognized Ann's people skills.

Although Ann loved her job, her ADD began to create problems from the start. She never developed an effective filing

10 IDEAL BOSS

(story continued)

system and soon was forced to waste long periods of time searching for memos and letters. Ann made typos and careless spelling errors (only some of which were caught by the computer's "spell checker"). She had little computer training and found the computer to be rather intimidating.

Any of these problems could have led to disaster, but no disaster occurred. Why? Because Ann had the good fortune to have an enlightened boss. The dean, as chance would have it, was familiar with the issues relating to ADD. She was also impressed with Ann's maturity, people skills, and forthright approach to stating her problems and seeking solutions.

Ann worked with another dean's assistant, to learn how to develop a better filing system. Ann attended classes to master the computer program she used on a daily basis. A student came in for several hours a week to assist Ann with typing and filing, thus allowing Ann to focus more comfortably on her people-related tasks.

The dean had found in Ann someone who could present a warm, professional, engaging face to the world, and helped her find the accommodations and supports she needed in order to concentrate on her strengths.

What were the characteristics of this boss that made her an ideal match for an ADD adult? The dean:

- Was supportive
- Was flexible
- Focused on her employee's strengths
- Understood the basis of ADD symptoms
- Was confident enough in her own position to work comfortably with an employee to find solutions

- Had no need for power struggles

- Respected her employee

- Was creative in finding solutions to problems

- Emphasized positive traits

"Okay," you might say, "but how many bosses are like Ann's?" Good question! Not most, unfortunately. However, thinking about Ann's boss can give you guidelines for some of the characteristics you'd like to find in a supervisor. You might not find someone with all the characteristics of Ann's boss, but you may have the good fortune to find someone who is flexible and motivated to learn how to best work with you.

Working with the Boss You Have

Don't expect your boss to figure you out. It's up to you to teach your boss how to best work with you. In other words, you have to know what you need and how you work best. When you are looking for a new job, your focus should be on finding a supervisor who you think will be a good match. If you already have a job, you need to help your supervisor understand you and your needs, and you need to teach him or her how to help you work most effectively.

Working Effectively with Your Boss

There are many positive, constructive ways to talk about your ADD symptoms and to work constructively with your boss to seek solutions. Here are some guidelines:

- Respect your boss's time and efforts. He or she has many responsibilities; supervising you is only one of them. Don't demand too much of your boss's time and energy. Regular, scheduled, focused, and brief supervisory sessions often are most effective.

- Don't let problems become enormous before you talk about them.

- If you mention your difficulties early—and in a positive, constructive fashion—they are less likely to become big problems.

- Don't just talk about these difficulties: Introduce possible solutions at the same time. Don't throw the problem into your boss's lap and expect him or her to solve it. You need to become informed enough about your ADD to propose reasonable solutions

- Unless you need an expensive or unusual accommodation, you may even decide it is best not to disclose an ADD diagnosis but to simply discuss problems and solutions in the context of the situation.

Searching for a More ADD-Friendly Boss

"How do I know what a new supervisor is really like until I work for him or her?" Job hunting is a two-way street. When you are interviewing for a new position, your prospective employer will do his or her best to find out about you—by reading your resume, talking with you, observing you, and speaking to your references. Employers do everything they can to make an accurate prediction about the type of employee an interviewee will become.

You need to engage in the same process. Don't just worry about whether they will like you. You also need to think about whether you will like them. You should do just as much research as your prospective employer in order to determine whether the job and the supervisor will be a good fit for you.

It's important for you to know what you're looking for and to feel comfortable asking questions about management style, the general atmosphere at work, turnover rate in the department, and the organizational structure of the company. If possible, find out whether the company is in the process of change; if there has been a merger or if one is anticipated in the near future, a change in structure and hierarchy is inevitable.

Use as many sources as you can to learn about your prospective employer. Look for friends or acquaintances who work for the firm or who know someone who does. Do some research in the library if you are considering a nationwide firm.

The Characteristics of Your Own Ideal Boss

When you are seeking the right boss, you should consider not only your ADD characteristics but also your personality in more general terms. Don't get so overfocused on your ADD symptoms that you overlook your personality, your interests, and your values. It is sometimes helpful to think about the Myers-Briggs personality types (see Chapter 6) when you try to imagine the type of person who would make an ideal boss for you. Entire books have been written about the Myers-Briggs Type Indicator (MBTI). It would be impossible within the confines of this chapter to offer a complete discussion of the MBTI (however, the discussion in Chapter 6 is a more complete one, and you may want to refer to it before continuing). Here, in the context of considering your ideal boss, we will limit our discussion to a narrow range of personality characteristics.

One of the most critical questions to ask yourself about any important relationship in your life—whether with a significant other or a supervisor—is this: Do you work best with someone who thinks like you or with someone whose strengths are complementary to yours? There are advantages and disadvantages to either choice.

Creativity versus Practicality

If you are inventive and creative and are always looking for new ways to do things, you may want to look for a supervisor with similar tendencies. In MBTI terms, this means that you are an intuitive (N) personality type and that you are seeking a supervisor who is an N also.

Many writers, intellectuals, scientists, professors, and other types of "idea people" are N's. Those people, with or without ADD, who are more oriented toward the world of the actual than the possible are sensing (S's) rather than intuitive (N's) individuals. The majority of people in the world are S's. S's are more focused on things that can be felt, touched, and worked with on a practical level. Whether doctors, nurses, engineers, mechanics, or teachers, they are focused on doing their job and improving their skills within the realm of what is already known. S's rarely stop to think about better ways of doing things; instead, they think in terms of maintaining current procedures in good working order.

If you are an N who is always trying to think of a better way to do things and you are supervised by an S who wants you to just buckle down and do your job, you may experience enormous frustration and tension in the workplace.

An S–N Workplace Vignette

> Marcus was a very creative ADD adult, a strong N on the MBTI. He was hired as a computer specialist in a large, conservative financial organization. The entire organization had a strong S orientation, concerned with preserving the status quo and doing things in a prescribed fashion.
>
> As a result of this enormous difference in orientation, Marcus experienced tremendous frustration each day. Marcus tried, in vain, to explain that things could be done more easily. His suggestions were unwelcome. "Just do your job!" was the attitude of his boss. Meanwhile, Marcus's ADD tendencies made the constant flow of detailed, repetitive paperwork barely supportable. His performance ratings went from mediocre to poor.
>
> Finally, through counseling Marcus came to terms with his boss's personality type. He developed a more patient attitude—while he actively looked for another position to which

(story continued)

he would be better suited. After several months of discrete explo-
ration, he found a person—another N like himself—who had
been placed in charge of developing new computer applica-
tions for the organization. A few months later, having smoothed
out the tension between himself and his current boss, he received
a good recommendation and was able to transfer to the more
compatible job situation.

Structure versus Flexibility

Another important parameter to consider in terms of both ADD and the
MBTI is your degree of comfort with structure. Don't confuse your difficulty in creating structure with your comfort or discomfort in having
structure! In other words, you may be a person whose ADD leads to
somewhat disorganized functioning but who prefers a certain degree of
structure. If so, you have a judging (J) rather than a perceiving (P) personality type and might work very well under the supervision of another
J who does not have ADD tendencies toward disorganization.

If you are a P with ADD—that is, an individual who finds too
much structure to be chafing and limiting—you may feel controlled
and micromanaged by a J boss. P's with ADD typically describe themselves as:

- Liking a great degree of freedom

- Disliking having to work regular hours

- Hating to work according to someone else's notions of how
  things should be done

Many P's with ADD prefer a more "laissez-faire" supervisory style, but may greatly benefit from structured assistance provided by support staff.

A P–J Workplace Vignette

Harold was a scientist with ADD and strong P tendencies who had worked in the academic world for many years, where his P tendencies were comfortably tolerated. As long as he showed up to teach his classes and attend faculty meetings, no one was concerned about his work hours. Harold was a night owl by nature (a common trait among people with ADD). A dedicated and highly creative person, he often worked all night long if he became really involved in an idea he was in the process of developing.

After a number of years in academia, Harold was hired by a private consulting firm. Harold was placed under the supervision of a strong J who had come to the consulting firm from the military—by definition, a strongly J environment, that is, one that values structure, hierarchy, predictability, and punctuality.

Under his J supervisor, Harold's productivity plummeted. Suddenly he was required to arrive at work by 8:30, even if he had been up until 2 or 3 working on a paper. His J boss was unable to understand why Harold preferred, and actually needed, to work on such a highly variable schedule.

He worked in his own style and at his own pace on evenings and weekends and spent his workday functioning as best he could under the chafing requirements of his J boss. His only hope was that his boss might move on within a year or two and then he might be left in peace by a more flexible supervisor.

Thinking versus Feeling

The thinking–feeling parameter on the MBTI is a critical one to consider in seeking a good match between yourself and your supervisor (as well as a match between yourself and your organization). What is the thinking–feeling parameter? In a general sense, T's are focused on detached, logical analysis in making value judgments while F's make value judgments along more personal dimensions. One might say that T's are more focused on non-people-related outcomes (such as research results, inventions, numbers, or income), whereas F's are only satisfied when the outcome of their efforts involves and benefits people directly. An F who works under a T might think that the T just doesn't care about people; the T, on the other hand, may think of the F as a "bleeding heart" or as someone quite impractical.

A T–F Workplace Vignette

An F worked under the supervision of a strong T in a social service organization. As is true for many social service organizations, this one was underfunded and understaffed. One day a dictate came down from a state-level administrator that a new software system was to be put into place, requiring that an enormous amount of data be reentered.

The T supervisor, a practical and nonsentimental sort, announced that, owing to the press of work demands, the traditional holiday party would consist of an early breakfast rather than the usual luncheon followed by early release from work. This decision was logical in view of the enormous work demands, but it completely ignored the "F" side of the equation—staff morale.

The F employee, a person with good people skills, was able to understand her supervisor's logic. She approached the supervisor on her own terms. She explained that although she understood the pressure the department was under to avoid turning a workday into a holiday she felt that in the long run the efficiency and productivity of staff members would decrease if they were deprived of this important time to relax, socialize, and enjoy the holiday spirit. The F point of view prevailed—because she was able to present her view in terms that could be appreciated by a T supervisor.

> **(story continued)**
>   *Whereas this T–F conflict was resolved in a positive fashion, many such conflicts are not resolved so amiably. For this reason, it is essential that you understand where you fall on the T–F dimension and think about this dimension carefully in choosing both an organization and a supervisor.*

Conclusion

As I have tried to demonstrate by using concepts from the MBTI, not every adult with ADD needs the same thing from a boss. There are some common ingredients, however. In general, you should look for someone who is tolerant of your weaknesses and appreciates your strengths, someone whose motives you trust, whom you feel comfortable communicating with, who can engage with you in creative problem-solving, and whose company you enjoy.

"But that's not who I work for!" you point out. First and foremost, you need to be realistic. Before you decide that you are in an intolerable situation, take a look at what you can change. You may be surprised by the changes you can bring about in your supervisor by changing your own attitude and approach. Stand back and consider (perhaps with the assistance of a counselor) how you can improve your relationship with your boss. Are there things you could do differently to improve your relationship with him or her (such as getting to work on time and arguing less frequently)? Have you presented your needs in a positive, problem-solving manner and indicated how motivated you are to improve your work performance? Are you positively motivated?

If after all your efforts, your relationship with your boss remains unsatisfactory, at least you'll have a better idea of what to look for in your next job.

This chapter discusses a range of workplace accommodations that may help to improve on-the-job functioning for individuals with ADD.

11

Reasonable
Workplace Accommodations

T he Americans with Disabilities Act (discussed in detail in Chapter 14) calls on employers to make "reasonable" accommodations for people with documented disabilities. It has not yet been clearly defined what accommodations are "reasonable" for persons with ADD. However, certain precedents are being set, and we are in the process of establishing a set of standards. This chapter attempts to list a number of accommodations that might be helpful to you in the workplace. Keep in mind, however, that this is merely a suggested list. Because something is suggested here does not mean that a court of law would require your employer to provide such accommodations. These decisions are made on a case-by-case basis. The needs and resources of the employer, as well as the needs of the employee, must be taken into account in determining what is reasonable. The list of accommodations in this chapter is meant to be used as a guideline as you try to develop a set of accommodations that are workable both for you and for your employer.

What Are Accommodations?

A ccommodations are methods, techniques, or approaches that can be used to enhance the functioning of a person with a disability. In the case of people with certain physical handicaps (e.g., paraplegics, the blind, the deaf), accommodations needed in the workplace are fairly easy to define and understand. In the case of invisible handicaps such as ADD or learning disabilities, however, necessary accommodations are less clear. An additional complication in the case of ADD is the fact that there is a wide range in the types and severity of symptoms.

How Do I Know What Types of Accommodations Would Be Helpful for Me?

We are now in the early stages of studying workplace accommodations for adults with ADD and/or learning disabilities. This chapter includes a list of suggested accommodations that have been useful to others. Accommodations for adults with ADD need to be devised on a case-by-case basis. The Job Accommodations Network,[1] a service of the President's Commission on the Employment of Persons with Disabilities, maintains a list of accommodations for persons with all types of disabilities. Some of the accommodations described here are included in the network's list of accommodations for individuals with learning disabilities; others are accommodations that were developed from my clinical experience.

Some accommodations are methods or techniques that you can provide for yourself. Others can be provided only by your employer. It may be most useful to work with an ADD expert as you attempt to work out a set of accommodations that will be the most appropriate for you in your particular workplace.

General Accommodations for ADD Adults in the Workplace

Changes in Supervisory Techniques

- ☐ Meet more frequently.
- ☐ Set short-term concrete goals.
- ☐ Give more emphasis to positive outcomes.

General Accommodations *(continued)*

☐ Clarify guidelines and job performance expectations.

☐ Provide frequent job performance reviews and use concrete, reasonable measures to assess improvement; give regular positive feedback as well.

☐ Evaluate employee in terms of strengths, not just weaknesses.

Changes in Job Description

☐ Remove from job descriptions particular tasks that cause the most difficulty.

☐ Increase proportion of tasks that are more closely suited to employees' strengths and interests.

Changes in Communication Patterns

☐ Provide more written communications.

☐ Communicate more frequently.

Changes in the Physical Work Environment

☐ Provide less distracting environment.

☐ Change lighting, work station, etc., to improve efficiency.

Use of "Assistive Technologies"

☐ Use tape recorder to record ideas and reminders.

☐ Use timers or beepers to assist with time management.

☐ Use computer software to assist with writing.

Provision of Specialized Training to Enhance Functioning

☐ Offer time management seminars.

☐ Offer seminars teaching organizational skills.

11 ACCOMMODATIONS

Symptom-Specific Accommodations for ADD

Distractibility

☐ Provide flashing light on phone (to be used instead of bell).

☐ Change location of work space to less distracting location.

☐ Permit use of meeting rooms, library, or another's private office, when available.

☐ Permit working at home for some defined fraction of the work week.

☐ Permit use of flextime, making it possible to work during the less distracting off-peak hours.

☐ Use a white noise machine to mask distracting sounds.

☐ Use headphones to mask distracting sounds.

☐ Permit closing office doors during certain time periods.

☐ Assign office mates with compatible work styles.

☐ Route phone calls to voice mail to minimize interruptions.

☐ Provide private office.

Hyperactivity

☐ Permit shift to job that allows more physical movement.

☐ Permit shift in work hours to allow extended exercise period at midday.

☐ Permit extended breaks several times a day for walking.

☐ Permit work in varied locations.

☐ Minimize need for participation in extended meetings.

☐ Provide table for employees who prefer to stand while working.

☐ Provide sufficient office space to allow pacing while working.

Symptom-Specific Accommodations *(continued)*

Difficulty with Organization/Planning/Follow-Through

☐ Provide possibility of teamwork with someone who can provide structure.

☐ Permit frequent face-to-face supervision.

☐ Provide means of sending frequent updates to supervisor— by voice mail, e-mail, or memo.

☐ Assist in breaking down long-term assignments into daily tasks.

☐ Provide training in time management and organization.

☐ Provide software to assist in scheduling and planning.

☐ Assist in devising an ADD-friendly filing system.

☐ Hire professional organizer or coach to organize physical office space (regular, repeated assistance is typically most useful).

☐ Reassign those with ADD to jobs that do not require supervision from others.

☐ Provide training in management and supervision if these duties are part of job description.

☐ Provide coach to assist those with ADD in ongoing development of better organizational skills.

☐ Provide checklists to give structure to multistage tasks.

☐ Provide regular assistance in prioritizing requests from multiple sources.

☐ Provide sample forms, letters, etc., to use as models.

Symptom-Specific Accommodations *(continued)*

Paperwork Problems

☐ Provide clerical support to handle paperwork.

☐ Reduce paperwork requirements.

☐ Provide coach to assist those with ADD in developing better paperwork techniques.

☐ Permit exchange of job duties with other workers (e.g., exchange phone duties for filing).

☐ Simplify forms and paperwork requirements.

Memory Difficulties

☐ Follow up verbal communications in writing.

☐ Make written communications clear and concise.

☐ Use video or audio equipment to record meetings.

☐ Provide training in memory enhancement.

☐ Train ADD employees in use of a day planner as a memory aid.

☐ Provide tape recorders so that employees can record reminders to themselves.

☐ Regularly post notices of events.

☐ Provide notes or minutes of meetings.

What Accommodations Is My Employer Required to Provide for Me?

If you have questions of a legal nature, you should refer to Chapter 14 to better understand what your employer is required to provide under the Americans with Disabilities Act.[2]

Keep in mind that as a general rule the primary responsibility for managing your ADD remains with you. Many approaches outlined in other chapters (see Chapters 3 and 4 on taking charge of your ADD) are steps you can take without the participation of your employer. Your employer and supervisor should be engaged in the process only when you have a need that cannot be met without their permission or cooperation.

How Should I Approach My Employer about Providing Accommodations?

Your employer is not required to provide any accommodations to you without a formal disclosure of a documented disability that is covered under the Americans with Disabilities Act (see Chapter 14). There are pros and cons to making such a disclosure (which are discussed in more detail in Chapter 14).

Often, the best approach is an informal request made in a positive, problem-solving manner. Present your difficulty to your supervisor, express your desire to function more efficiently, and suggest the accommodation that would help you do so. For example: "I have the problem of being easily distracted by sounds. Ever since we purchased the new high-speed copy machine, I have noticed that I have much more difficulty concentrating at my desk. If it is possible, I would like to have the location of my cubicle changed to a spot further from the copy center so that I can be more productive." Your supervisor may respond that he or she cannot grant special favors to you and that such a change could only be made on the basis of a documented disability. In this instance, you will have to decide whether the advantages of disclosing your disability outweigh the disadvantages of such a disclosure. Your supervisor may say that such a move isn't feasible at the moment but that when an anticipated reorganization takes place, he or she will keep your request in mind. In this instance your request for accommodations may be granted without official disclosure of your disability.

11 ACCOMMODATIONS

Conclusion

R eminder: Don't rely on your employer to take responsibility for accommodations. Be proactive. You must always take charge of your ADD needs. Many of the accommodations described in this chapter are things you can provide for yourself or can arrange for yourself. If you must look to your employer to accommodate you, it remains your responsibility to understand your needs and present them to your employer. Make reasonable requests for accommodations that are compatible with the overall functioning of the organization.

What's good for ADD is good for the organization. Everyone struggles with some of the symptoms associated with ADD—absentmindedness, distractibility, disorganization, and difficulties with verbal memory and decision making. Employees with ADD strongly need accommodations, but everyone can potentially benefit from them. For example, one woman with ADD worked in real estate sales. The forms she was expected to complete following each sale were complicated and poorly designed. As a way to cope with her ADD paperwork problems, she developed a simplified form for herself that was soon in widespread use among her non-ADD coworkers!

Employers who become more sensitive and responsive to the needs of those with ADD will find that in the process of improving the efficiency of their ADD employees they have developed approaches that improve the overall efficiency of the organization, thus creating a win–win situation.

IN
THIS
CHAPTER

For some adults with ADD, an office environment will never be their optimum workplace, no matter what accommodations may be available. This chapter describes some alternatives, such as telecommuting, self-employment, and multiple part-time jobs.

12

Alternatives to a "9-to-5" Job

Section One—Custom Designing Your Own Work Life

If you are one of those adults with ADD who has always felt "hemmed in," frustrated, or "asleep at the wheel" when working in an office; who has always dreamed of working for yourself, of starting your own business, and of getting out of the commuter lanes, then this is the chapter for you! By working for yourself, or in partnership with someone else, you have a much greater range of choices to custom design your work life. This chapter discusses a range of possible choices and also talks of ways to make your workday productive and your home office as "ADD-friendly" as possible.

Doing What You Love . . .

Of all the work-related choices you can make as an adult with ADD, the most important one is to choose to do something you really love. It is a well-established fact that people with ADD cannot only focus, but at times can hyperfocus on activities that really engage and intrigue them. By choosing to do something that really interests you, and by carefully designing your working life to optimize your energy and effectiveness, your likelihood of success is tremendously enhanced.

In her book, *Making a Living Without a Job*, Barbara Winter writes of the importance of earning a living by being ourselves and by having fun at what we're doing.[1]

Another writer, Marsha Sinetar, author of *Do What You Love, the Money Will Follow*, describes patterns that sound remarkably like those of adults with ADD,[2] although her comments are directed toward the general public. She writes that when people are bored, frustrated, or constrained by the work they do all day, they are plagued by drifting attention. By contrast, when a person is totally absorbed in a task and can bring his or her full attention to it, he or she becomes most effective. The process Sinetar is describing is one so crucial to becoming an effective person with ADD—to find what engages us, what intrigues us, and then to take advantage of our ADD ability to hyperfocus.

Acknowledging Your Need for Stimulation and Variety

If you are considering developing your own business, or perhaps pursuing a number of activities from a home-based office, don't let yourself be overly influenced by the "nay sayers." Adults with ADD are often highly successful in very nontraditional ways. Doing several things at once, or doing several different things in fairly rapid succession may be highly suitable for an adult with ADD, who needs challenge, pressure, variety, and stimulation to perform optimally. Such approaches may seem foolhardy or too risky to those without ADD tendencies.

In her book, Barbara Winter writes of a young man who was not diagnosed with ADD but whose pattern resembled many people with ADD. He spoke of having lots of ideas and lots of projects. Rather than fearing and focusing on failure, this young man thought of his life like a juggler. "You get lots of plates spinning. If one of them crashes, you just go on to the next one. Not all of your ideas are going to work, and even your best ideas may not last. But that isn't the measure of success."[3] This young man recognized his need for change, stimulation, and risk taking and did not consider himself a failure if not all of his attempts met with success or developed into long-term enterprises.

Thom Hartmann talks of planning—actually expecting and accommodating his need to move on to new projects.[4] He, like many adults with ADD, loves to be creative and innovative. He conceives new projects and new products and finds great excitement in bringing his ideas into reality. After this highly stimulating and creative phase, Thom knows he will lose interest and motivation. Rather than seeing this as a negative, he plans for someone with different skills and interests to take over the day-to-day management of his enterprises once he gets them off the ground. Thom describes himself and similar adults with ADD as "hunters" living in a world of "farmers"—adults who can function in work that is slow, predictable, and repetitive. While ADD "hunters" crave stimulation, challenge, and risk, "farmers" desire stability with minimal risk or challenge.

As an adult with ADD, you should understand your differences and take them seriously. Thom Hartmann warns ADD adults, or "hunters," not to allow the "farmers" of the world to set the standards by which they judge themselves. The distractibility and inability of those with ADD to function at their best increases when they are required to do dull, unsatisfying work. However, their ability to hyperfocus, to live in the moment, and to become totally involved in a project is greater than that of the "farmers." Often, by working for themselves, ADD adults have the freedom to choose work that will turn their ADD energy and hyperfocusing ability into a great gift.

Ideal work conditions for many adults with ADD:

- A high-interest activity
- An optimal degree of pressure
- Relative autonomy
- Flexibility in tasks and timetables

12 ALTERNATIVE JOBS

- An option to move on to new projects as interest wanes
- A minimum of administrative responsibilities

Why "9-to-5" Might Not Work for All Adults with ADD

When most of us think of work, we tend to think of a standard, 9-to-5 job in an office environment, employed by someone else. By definition, when we are an employee, it is the employer who sets the agenda, the priorities, and the schedule. Some adults with ADD, however, find that they need a much greater degree of flexibility and choice than can be found in the 9-to-5 world. An office environment may not be very ADD-friendly for a number of reasons:

- 9-to-5 may not be your optimal work hours.
- An "open" office environment may be too distracting.
- An office job may involve too much paperwork.
- Desk work may not allow enough physical movement.
- The job may involve too much work that is uninteresting, repetitive, and overly detailed.
- The job may involve long-term projects in which an adult with ADD may lose interest long before they are finished.
- Office politics may prove frustrating and difficult.
- Corporate culture or management style may be a mismatch.

Looking at Alternatives to a "9-to-5" Existence

For individuals with ADD one of the great advantages of reaching adulthood is that your range of choices expands. In high school you perhaps had very few alternatives. If you went to college, you most likely found a wider range of choices. The range of choice often becomes greater still once you enter the world of work. There are many alternatives to a 9-to-5 job. Some of those alternatives include:

- Telecommuting, part-time or full-time
- Home-based business
- Independent professional practice
- Multiple part-time jobs
- Independent artistic or creative activities
- Entrepreneurial activities
- Consulting

Matching Alternative Solutions to Problems

If you are unhappy in your current work environment and would like to make a change, you should carefully consider which aspects of the office environment are "ADD-unfriendly" for you and then consider possible solutions. These solutions could range from keeping your current job while telecommuting from home on a part-time basis, having a part-time job that allows you time to develop other income-producing activities, or taking the plunge and working for yourself full-time.

Each of the alternatives listed in the previous section entails pluses and minuses for adults with ADD. So in order to make a good alternative work choice:

❶ Carefully consider the pros and cons of each alternative.

❷ Make a realistic self-assessment asking yourself:

Under what work conditions am I happiest?

What is most likely to make me productive and effective?

What are my likely downfalls?

❸ Problem-solve to minimize or avoid any downfalls.

Telecommuting

Edna Murphy, in her book, *Flexible Work*,[5] writes that more and more companies are opting for telecommuting for selected employees. She describes the ideal telecommuter as:

- Output oriented

- Self-disciplined

- Trusted by managers

- Well organized

- A good time manager

- Self-aware, who knows his or her own needs

- Able to seek help when appropriate

- Content with little interaction with coworkers, gaining more satisfaction from the work itself

- Seeking a better balance between home and work life

At first glance, this list may seem to rule out adults with ADD as telecommuters! Self-disciplined, well organized, and good time managers? These are often pitfalls, not strengths, for ADDers. But don't immediately discount the idea. To decide whether working from home on a part-time basis might be constructive for you, take a look at some of the "pluses" and "minuses" from an ADD perspective.

"Pluses" of Telecommuting

Elimination of office distractions

The possibility of taking breaks when needed

Working time-shifted hours when preferable—telecommuting is often good for ADD "night owls"

The opportunity to exercise during the day to reduce fidgetiness and restlessness

A chance to be more available to children and spouse during afternoon and early evening

Elimination of time wasted by commuting

The opportunity to dress casually and comfortably

"Minuses" of Telecommuting

The distractions of home: television, projects around the house, other activities

Less structure or guidance on what to do or when to do it

No external cues to remain on task, organized, and focused

The tendency to sleep late or to procrastinate without the structure of a workplace environment

Loneliness, isolation

Interruptions by family

If you would like to consider telecommuting, you need to be honest in your self-evaluation and make efforts to reduce or eliminate the "minuses."

Some ways to stay "on track" as an ADD telecommuter include:

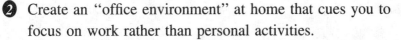

1 Develop rituals and structured times to work.

2 Create an "office environment" at home that cues you to focus on work rather than personal activities.

3 Check in by phone at the office when you sit down at your desk—this cues both you and your work colleagues that you are "at work."

4 Verbalize deadlines to coworkers.

5 Have a regular e-mail communication at day's end with your supervisor to update him or her on your day's accomplishments.

6 Set daily goals.

Telecommuting schedules can vary widely. Some telecommuters do the great majority of their work at home and may only go to

12 ALTERNATIVE JOBS

the office for specific meetings with colleagues or supervisors. Other telecommuters, like Angela, whose story is described below, chose telecommuting as a part-time option best suited for work activities that required extended concentration.

Angela, a Part-Time Telecommuter

Angela was an adult with ADD who worked for a small nonprofit organization. It was Angela's job to develop themes for conferences held by her organization and to oversee the planning and coordination of those conferences. Her work involved travel, as well as a great deal of writing. She loved the variety and stimulation of her work but found that she had enormous difficulty concentrating in close quarters at the office. As she tried to write, telephones were ringing on adjacent desks and coworkers frequently interrupted her to ask questions or to make comments.

Angela was able to negotiate with her boss to become a part-time telecommuter. She set up an organized office space at home, including computer, e-mail, telephone, and fax. She made a regular time schedule in her home office to work on those things that required sustained concentration and made herself available by phone, e-mail, and fax for ready interface with her colleagues. This arrangement provided a good solution for her distractibility, while still allowing communication with her colleagues.

Operating a Home-Based Business

While a home-based business entails many of the ADD challenges of telecommuting it includes additional challenges that telecommuters do not have to face. Telecommuters still have ties to an employer who can provide some degree of support and structure. They also are in touch with colleagues, have tasks and deadlines set by others, must meet expectations set by others, and usually have the benefit of support staff and equipment at the office. A telecommuter coordinates her or his work with others. These connections provide a degree of structure and pressure to stay on-task.

When you operate a home-based business, you have less support and structure and fewer connections with coworkers. Instead you have an operation that requires a greater range of activities and responsibilities and a much greater degree of independence. It is you who sets the goal, the agenda, the structure, and the pace. Let's look at Mary's story and why she encountered difficulties in her home-based business.

Mary, the Avon Lady

Mary was a woman with ADD who was married and had three children. She had sold Avon products on a part-time basis for several years and decided to try her hand at developing a home-based full-time Avon business.

Mary, like many adults with ADD, was a night owl who greatly resisted getting up in the mornings. When she had worked outside the home, she had no choice but to get up. As an "Avon Lady" she found herself sleeping later. As a result, mornings in her household became chaotic.

With no structure to her day, Mary found that she spent the first couple of hours each morning drinking coffee, reading through the paper, and watching the morning television shows. She reasoned that calling people before 10 A.M. was too early. What Mary didn't do was use these hours to do household chores, work-related paperwork, or planning.

Her small house did not afford her the luxury of a separate office space. She used a small desk in the kitchen to make phone calls and record orders. This desk was usually piled high, and papers often became mixed with the day's mail and the chil-

> *(story continued)*
> dren's school papers. Her dining room became the storage area
> and staging ground for bagging individual Avon orders.
>
> Mary found that she loved the social aspect of house
> calls and phone calls but typically spent more time socializing
> than selling. Orders often had to be delivered in the evenings,
> since many of her clients were employed full-time. As a result,
> her evenings became more confused—in addition to dinner
> preparation and homework, she was now making Avon deliv-
> eries at a time when her family commitments were at their
> highest.
>
> Three years later, after many battles with her husband
> over financial difficulties and chaos at home, Mary reluctantly
> agreed to return to her former job as a receptionist. Mary loved
> the freedom, flexibility, and sociability of being a full-time Avon
> Lady but reluctantly came to realize that she had not devel-
> oped disciplined patterns that would allow her to be successful
> in this kind of endeavor. She finally concluded that, for her, the
> schedule and structure of an office job were necessary for her
> to stay focused.

Although a home-based business did not work for Mary, this
does not mean that it cannot work for you. Home-based businesses
seem to work best for people with ADD when:

① They work with someone else. This can be a spouse, a
partner, or even an employee. Interfacing with others to
keep the business running provides a degree of focus and
structure.

② They have a separate area of the home from which to run
their business. This area can be a basement, a garage that has
been converted, or even a spare bedroom.

They establish a routine. This routine does not have to be a "standard" daytime work hours routine but needs to be a disciplined routine that is not subject to procrastination or the constant invasion of personal or family activities.

④ They hire someone or work in partnership with someone who can handle the parts of the business that are most difficult for them. This typically includes paperwork, billing, filing, and record keeping.

⑤ They focus on their strengths—often in the area of sales, marketing, creative innovations, and product development.

Independent Professional Practice

Professionals with ADD often find that they are more content to work for themselves rather than in large practices or organizations. Whether they are doctors, lawyers, psychologists, financial advisors, or in other professions, adults with ADD typically prefer the autonomy and independence of a small or independent practice. Let's look at three scenarios.

(Mis)Managing a Medical Practice

Alan was an internist with never formally diagnosed ADD. In the process of his daughter's evaluation for ADD, his wife immediately recognized very strong ADD traits in her husband. Although he was in the range of superior intelligence, he had always been highly scattered and disorganized. Alan, however, was unwilling to consider the possibility that he, too, had ADD. Alan's denial of ADD became the "last straw" in an already heavy burden borne by his wife.

Concluding that he had no intention of looking at himself and trying to change destructive patterns, she decided to leave the marriage. In the process of the separation, she also

12 ALTERNATIVE JOBS

(story continued)
resigned from being his nurse and office manager. For years she had kept his schedule, reminded him of deadlines and events, and nagged him to keep up with paperwork and dictation. Despite all of her efforts, however, the office was a shambles. He typically came home with a foot-high pile of charts, resolving to catch upon his dictations, only to fall asleep in front of the television yet again.

Following the separation, Alan's practice quickly deteriorated to an unworkable situation. Overwhelmed by the organizational tasks of running an independent private practice, he sold his practice and took position within a large managed care organization in his community.

From Teacher to Real Estate Agent

Scott was a very gifted teacher whose ADD helped him to be very dynamic and creative in the classroom, although grading papers and record keeping had always been a tremendous struggle. He and his wife, a fellow teacher, wanted to have children and concluded that two teachers' salaries could not comfortably support a family. Scott, a personable, high-energy individual, decided to go into real-estate sales.

One year later, however, Scott sought counseling. He felt anxious, depressed, and very disturbed with his lack of success as a real estate agent. He described his days as drifting and unfocused. After his wife left in the morning for her teaching job, he found himself procrastinating, watching television, going to the local gym, walking the dog—almost anything except drum-

(story continued)

ming up business. He disliked making cold calls, detested the detailed paperwork.

Through counseling, Scott recognized that the isolation and complete lack of structure of his day were paralyzing for him. He resolved to schedule time each day at the real estate office, manning the phones, making contacts with potential clients, and learning ways to build his client base from fellow agents. Scott also decided to apprentice himself to another agent, accompanying him on calls with clients. Scott learned through his counseling and the positive results from the changes he made that he needed the support provided by mentoring and the structure provided by regular hours spent in the office.

Barry, an Independent Financial Consultant

Barry had arranged a professional life for himself in which he found both personal satisfaction and financial success. Let's look carefully at the differences between his approach and theirs. In studying these differences you may find some clues to structuring a successful professional practice for yourself as an adult with ADD.

Barry was a highly independent financial consultant whose consulting practice thrived. What did he do differently from Scott and Alan? Primarily Barry was able to see himself realistically, with detachment and accuracy and to make changes in his work life accordingly.

Early in his career, he had worked in a large brokerage firm that he found constraining to work for.

12 ALTERNATIVE JOBS

(story continued)

  In his mid-thirties he decided to take the plunge and open his own private office. Realistic about his strengths, he knew that he excelled at developing a client base, in inspiring confidence in those clients, and in making strong recommendations for investment opportunities. Equally realistic about his ADD traits, he recognized the need to establish order, flexibility, and low stress in his work environment. He rented office space a scant ten minutes from his home. Knowing his weakness in the areas of paperwork and record keeping, he wisely convinced his administrative assistant in the large firm to move with him to his private firm. She already had an in-depth knowledge of the business and of record keeping needs and procedures.

  Barry created a work environment in which he was in charge, which gave him the flexibility to take breaks during the day when they were needed, and to keep his work flow at a manageable level. He was also realistic about the amount of work required to run an independent consulting firm. He worked very hard but on a schedule that suited his own biological rhythms. He taught his adminstrative assistant to protect him from unnecessary interruptions and to handle as much of the administrative portion of the work without involving him.

  Barry's business was soon thriving. Although he could have easily expanded by taking on associates and creating a bustling financial advising service, he was smart enough to realize that he didn't want to re-create an environment similar to that which he had voluntarily left a number of years earlier. After fifteen years of independent work, he had created the ideal life for himself, earning a comfortable living, keeping his stress level low, and recognizing his limitations as well as his strengths.

Multiple Part-Time Jobs

Having two or more part-time jobs can sometimes be an ideal solution for an adult with ADD. By working for others in these part-time jobs, the structure and time lines are built-in. By having more than one job, there is more movement and variety, which helps prevent the boredom and restlessness that so often plague adults with ADD in the workplace.

Wayne, Have Social Work Degree, Will Travel

Wayne was a clinical social worker with ADD who arranged a work schedule that kept him interested and active. Initially, after earning his degree, he found a full-time job in a social service agency. There he found that the work was repetitive, the work load was stressful, and a great percentage of his time was taken up with paperwork. All of these are warning signals for adults with ADD. After a couple of years, Wayne felt very dissatisfied and began to search for work alternatives.

Changes in his work life evolved gradually. At first he accepted part-time work in the evening, in an agency that dealt with the elderly. There he co-led a counseling group for people in retirement homes. He found he enjoyed the interpersonal interaction as well as the very low demand for paperwork. He was well liked and was offered more work over the next several months. Through his professional grapevine he learned of part-time work of a similar nature available at a large private agency that dealt with the needs of the elderly.

Over the course of a year, Wayne resigned from his full-time job, having been able to arrange two part-time jobs offering him equal pay and greater satisfaction. Because he was not a member of the full-time staff of either agency, his presence was normally not required at administrative meetings, allowing him

(story continued)

to focus on the clinical work that he loved. He enjoyed the variety of going to different work sites on different days, the reduced paperwork requirements, and the stimulation of a variety of professional activities.

Anne, Two Part-Time Jobs, Two Careers

Anne was a trained nurse who loved working with and helping people, but she was very unhappy in the managed health care environment where she was employed. A highly trained, highly intelligent woman, she found that the high stress and lack of autonomy in her workplace were having a very negative effect on her attitude and professional satisfaction.

Through some creative problem solving in counseling, Anne decided to take a risk and give up her frustrating, but highly secure job in order to seek greater personal satisfaction. She was hired as a part-time clinical supervisor to younger, less-experienced visiting nurses in the community. Anne loved the opportunity to pass on the knowledge gained by her years of experience as well as the recognition and respect she gained as an instructor and supervisor.

At the same time, she found an outlet for her love of writing, something she had pursued in college but had found no time for when employed as a full-time nurse. She was hired half-time to work on a nursing newsletter, editing and writing articles. This gave her a much-desired intellectual outlet and gave her the opportunity to express ways in which she felt her profession needed to be changed.

Anne exchanged an inflexible full-time job for two very different part-time jobs, both of which offered her intellectual

(story continued)
stimulation and challenge. In both of these positions she not only had structure and interaction but also a high degree of autonomy and variety—often an ideal combination for an adult with ADD.

Creative Activities at Home

Have you ever dreamed of writing the Great American Novel, of pursuing the artistic talent you've ignored since high school or college, of really developing your skills as a potter, weaver, or other type of craftsperson. For some adults with ADD, the urge to create and the satisfaction of creative activity is one of their strongest driving forces.

The pros and cons are very similar to any type of work that you might pursue at home on a completely independent basis: how to keep yourself focused and how to meet your needs for structure, administrative support, and social contact, without detracting from your work at home.

Larry, an ADD Photographer

Larry was a highly talented photographer whose home-based photography business fell apart when his non-ADD wife, Lynn, grew tired of dedicating her life to keeping him focused. For a number of years, she had been his business manager, taking care of advertising, marketing, and serving as his agent in setting up photography exhibits. He became well-known in his community for his intuitive, highly personal portraits as well as for more abstract, artistic photography. When Lynn gave up being his support system, Larry's business rapidly faltered.

(story continued)

Unlike Barry, the financial consultant, he had no experience in establishing supports for himself. He had married his support system, and his support system had resigned.

Through counseling with the couple, Lynn agreed to return to working with him on a limited-time basis and to helping him to "grow up" professionally by finding and hiring the necessary supports to replace her. During the course of the next year, Larry found a photography assistant who also had good organizational skills. He also located an agent to promote his gallery work. Eventually with his assistant's and agent's support, Larry's business grew. He developed a line of note cards featuring his photographs and found a publisher to print a calendar of scenes he had photographed of the local Pennsylvania countryside. Two years after Lynn's final "resignation," Larry found that he had, in fact, been able to build a professional support system that functioned even better than his former overdependence on his wife.

Michael, Novelist or On-Line Addict?

Michael was an adult with ADD who worked as a technical writer in the computer industry. He enjoyed the opportunity for travel that his work afforded him and worked well under the publishing deadlines. Michael, however, had always dreamed of writing fiction. An English major in college, he had found work as a technical writer as a practical move after graduation. When the industry newsletter for which he worked was bought out by a larger newsletter, Michael's job was eliminated. Rather than looking for another position, Michael and his wife, Anne, decided to let this become an opportunity for him

(story continued)

to pursue his dream. Anne's recent promotion allowed them more financial flexibility. They decided that Michael would stay home and work on his novel, begun several years earlier and gathering dust in a corner.

One year later, however, Michael found himself anxious and depressed. With medication and with the structure of deadlines and short-term projects, he had functioned well. Now, at home full-time, with no structure, no social contact, and no deadlines, Michael found himself sleeping late, struggling with writer's block, and spending more and more of his time writing e-mail messages to other lonely people. Hungry for personal contact, his social world became interaction with others he had "met" on-line.

Through counseling, Michael recognized that having "all the time in the world" to write was not an advantage for him. Rather than give up his dream of completing his novel, he decided to do two things to give more structure to his day. First, he recontacted former colleagues in the technical writing field and found a part-time job. This job got him up in the morning, gave him some social contact, and lent structure to his workweek. Secondly, he joined a writer's group. In this group, each writer brought ongoing work to share and critique. This way, he found that he kept more focused when writing. He had only a limited number of hours each week in which to write, and he had a group that was expecting to hear about his progress on a weekly basis. Thus, through some trial and error, Michael finally found a working combination of flexibility and structure that allowed him to be focused and productive in pursuing his dream of fiction writing.

12 ALTERNATIVE JOBS

Entrepreneur

Thom Hartmann writes that some adults with ADD are ideally suited to be entrepreneurs.[6] Such people, he finds, are risk takers, who are easily bored by mundane activities. Hartmann believes that ADD adults are overrepresented in the population of entrepreneurs because they can be so ideally suited to this type of high risk, high stimulation activity. While not all adults with ADD fit Hartmann's hunter model, if you feel that his hunter traits describe you, then you may want to consider engaging in some sort of entrepreneurial activity yourself.

The types of entrepreneurial activities Hartmann refers to are more challenging because they are self-generated, more creative, less structured, and may involve more risk in terms of initial investment of time and money.

One of the big ADD pitfalls of starting your own business is that typically, at the outset, you don't have the capital to hire others to help you, forcing you to perform tasks for which you may be poorly suited, due to your ADD.

Thom Hartmann also writes of another interesting phenomenon among entrepreneurs with ADD.[7] He finds that he, and many others, are more excited by and suited to the creation of a new enterprise but ill suited to managing its day-to-day operations. Once the "hunter" is faced with "farmer" managerial activities, which require repetition, persistence, regularity, and patience, he loses interest. In his own life, Thom expects this to happen and plans for a transition in which he hands over the managerial reins to someone else while he moves on to a new and exciting project.

Consulting

Kate Kelly and Peggy Ramundo, both adults with ADD and authors of *You Mean I'm Not Lazy, Stupid or Crazy?!*, point out that for adults with ADD, the life of a consultant may provide the best of both worlds: the more structured world of the corporate office environment and the flexible world of the self-employed. They state, "As a consultant . . . it can be easier to avoid arbitrary rules and rigid people. You can . . . move on when policies and people start getting on your nerves." At the same time, they note that you can "retain some of the benefits of working for someone else—use of office equipment, secretarial support and the established network of business contacts."[8]

Unlike a new entrepreneur, a consultant is working with a familiar set of skills he or she has already developed and is often working with people with whom he or she already has a long-established relationship. For these reasons, there is more familiarity and more built-in structure. Consultants can command high hourly wages as experts in their field without having to struggle with the non-ADD-friendly responsibilities of serving as a manager within a large firm.

As with all of the variants of more independent work life that have been discussed in this chapter, the downside of consulting is often related to administrative details. Many adults with ADD describe that the consulting work itself is very satisfying. They find that generating ideas and verbal communication are easy for them. However, the necessary follow-up reports, record keeping, and billing can be their downfall.

Section Two: Tools for Success in Self-Created Jobs

In the first section of this chapter a variety of alternatives to a "9-to-5" job have been explored, considering the pros and cons of each alternative. No matter which alternative you might be considering, there are a number of patterns, techniques, or approaches that may make your efforts to custom design your work life more likely to succeed.

Creating Your Own Support Network

If you choose to work independently, one of the most effective ways to combat the negative effects of your ADD is to create a "team" or support network around you. Who is part of this network and how elaborate it is depends upon your needs and activities.

Support staff. Many consultants, home-based business people, or professionals starting out in independent practice protest that they cannot afford support staff. If you have ADD, the reality is more likely that you can't afford *not to* have support. This doesn't mean that you must hire a full-time assistant. There are many creative ways to meet your needs without overextending yourself financially. There are many people with professional secretarial skills who have their own home-based business and can work for you on an hourly basis doing all kinds of administrative work—typing, record keeping, billing, tax reports, etc. They don't even need to come to your office. With the convenience of answering machines, fax machines, and E-mail it is quite possible to stay in close touch without being physically in the same environment.

Partnerships. Another way to create a support network is to form a partnership. Some adults with ADD find that having a partner or partners in their enterprises helps to keep them on track and gives them a forum for processing new ideas as well as a way to divide work according to the skills and preferences of the partners. Even less formally, it is possible to work in partnership with one or more people on specific projects without forming a legal partnership.

Support groups for the self-employed. Many self-employed individuals who work out of their homes, whether they have ADD or not, feel isolated and hungry for interaction with other home-based self-employed people. In several cities, clubs have sprung up in response to this need. In Washington, D.C., for example, there is a small group of self-employed professionals who meet regularly for lunch. This affords them social stimulation of a professional nature and allows them to share experiences, problems, and solutions. In the process, some of these professionals have formed contacts with one another that have enhanced their work projects.

You may find that some or all of these approaches for forming a support network are helpful to you in developing and maintaining your independent work life. What seems clear, however, is that most adults with ADD seem to function better when they have the opportunity to get feedback, share ideas, build structure, and delegate non-ADD-friendly tasks to employees, contractors, or partners.

Tools for Managing Your Time and Work at Home

Merrill and Donna Douglass, in their book *Manage Your Time, Your Work, Yourself*,[9] outline a range of techniques for enhancing personal effectiveness and productivity on the job. Some of their excellent ideas are included in the following discussion.

Time Management—Peak Hours and "Pit" Hours

The more independently you work, the more important good time-management skills become. This doesn't mean inflexibility, but it does mean discipline. Know yourself, your peak performance hours, and your "pit" performance hours. Schedule your at-home work accordingly.

Planning and Scheduling

You should make a plan for each day, either at the end of the previous workday or as you begin your new workday. According to Donna and Merrill Douglass many people erroneously use planning and scheduling interchangeably. However, there is an important difference:

Planning is what you are going to do.

Scheduling is when you are going to do it.

After you have made your plan for the day, then schedule when, and in what order, you are going to carry out your plan. A plan doesn't have to be inflexible. If circumstances change, don't give up your plan; rather, alter your plan according to the unforeseen events, and then proceed with the altered plan.

"To Do" Lists

Make your "to do" lists work for you, but don't become a slave to them. Some adults with ADD become so overfocused on making daily task lists that they become overwhelmed by an overly lengthy and detailed list. Others play mental games, pretending that each item on the list is of equal value. They then proceed to do all of the "easy" items, whether or not they are important, because they feel so satisfied by the numerous items they have been able to check off. Meanwhile, the most critical task of the day, most likely a multistep, challenging task, goes undone.

To make the most of a "to do" list:

1 Write a realistic, doable list.

2 Take care of items on that list in order of importance.

3 Take advantage of odd moments that might otherwise be wasted to take care of the quick and easy "to do" items, rather than beginning your day with them.

Make Your Moods Work *for* You

Many adults with ADD report that they can only work when they are "in the mood." They may sound petulant, almost childish, when saying "I'm not in the mood" to work, and you may find yourself feeling this way at times. However, don't use your moods as an excuse not to work. Use your moods as a powerful engine that can drive great productivity. Shift from task to task as your mood and energy level change. When you work at home, you have much greater flexibility. Write during your peak hours, then do more mundane tasks as your energy level falls. Schedule necessary meetings or business-related errands for times when you feel restless or energy depleted.

Procrastination

Procrastination is often a struggle for adults with ADD, even in a structured office environment. The possibilities for procrastination multiply with a home-based workplace, where little or no external structure is provided, and there are few, if any, people to report to. If you tend to be a procrastinator, you need to work even harder to develop "anti-procrastination tools," particularly if you are considering working at home. Here are some approaches that can help:

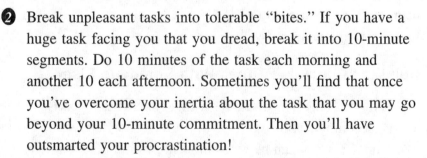

1. Do the unpleasant stuff first. For many, filing is one of those tasks that gets put off. They find that if they leave it to the end of their workday, they're likely to tell themselves, "I'm tired. I'll do it tomorrow." But by starting your day with filing, you can create order so that you can work more efficiently for the remainder of the day.

2. Break unpleasant tasks into tolerable "bites." If you have a huge task facing you that you dread, break it into 10-minute segments. Do 10 minutes of the task each morning and another 10 each afternoon. Sometimes you'll find that once you've overcome your inertia about the task that you may go beyond your 10-minute commitment. Then you'll have outsmarted your procrastination!

3. Set a deadline and make it known to others. Make verbal commitments to others. Saying "I'll fax that report to you by the end of the day" makes it more likely to happen.

④ Promise yourself a reward. Give yourself something to look forward to. Tell yourself, I'll take a walk, call a friend, or get a snack, after I've written that letter. Be sure to make the reward immediate. It will motivate you more.

⑤ Delegate. There may be tasks so burdensome to you that it is much smarter to delegate that task to someone else. In a home-based business, this usually means hiring an assistant or specialist. You may protest, "But I can't afford that expense!" In some instances you can't afford not to.

Tips for Making Your Independent Workday Productive

Get an Early Start

"As your first hour goes, so goes the rest of the day!" Remember that "It's the early bird who catches the worm." Don't give in to the temptation to sleep in, read the paper for an hour, or otherwise put off starting your workday just because you don't have a boss looking over your shoulder. You'll most likely find you are more productive if you take breaks later in the day when your concentration wanes, rather than "goofing off" at the beginning.

Begin (or End) Your Day with a Planning Session

During this session review your daily task list, and schedule when you plan to accomplish each task (or cluster of tasks). Use this time for longer-term planning as well.

Build in "Check-in" Times With Someone Else

Normally this check-in would be with a colleague, supervisor (if you are a telecommuter), or partner. If you are completely solo in your work, this check-in can be with someone who is functioning as your ADD coach, an assistant, or your spouse. These check-ins should help you keep on track. Talk about what you plan to accomplish that day or what you have accomplished.

Identify Personal Temptations and Distractions

- Identify your personal temptations. These might include television watching, reading the paper, talking on the phone, playing computer games, or going "on-line" to interact with others.

- Develop solutions to limit these temptations. Make a rigid rule: "No TV" during your specified work hours. Alternatively, use these temptations as rewards for completing work-related tasks that are unappealing to you.

Set Boundaries for Yourself Between Personal and Work Life

One of the advantages of working for yourself, or working at home, is that you can more conveniently take care of personal and family business during the week. Make sure this advantage doesn't become a pitfall, however, by consistently robbing you of time you intended to devote to your work. It may help to schedule "personal time," for example, set aside designated parts of your day or parts of your week for appointments, grocery shopping, chores, etc.

If you have the necessary time awareness and self-discipline, you may choose to move back and forth between professional activities and personal activities throughout your day, choosing to exercise, work in the garden, or prepare a meal as a break from your work activities when you find that your concentration is waning. The key here is to manage those breaks so that an intended half-hour break doesn't grow into extended, unintended time away from your work.

Set Boundaries for Your Family Between Work and Personal Life

It is important for your spouse and children to realize that just because you're home doesn't mean you're not "at work." Your spouse may assume that you are the obvious choice for running errands during the day since he or she is "at work" and you are "at home." Of course they are less likely to respect work/personal life boundaries if you don't. If you are prone to watch Oprah in the afternoon when you intended to be working, you are certainly inviting your spouse or children to request that you pick up the dry cleaning, run to the store, or drive the car pool!

The issues for young children who have a working parent at home should also be addressed. It is difficult for young children to understand and accept that even though their mother or father is at home, they cannot be disturbed or spoken to because they are "working." One psychotherapist whose office was at home told a humorous story of his four-year-old daughter who came running stark naked into his consulting room where he was seeing a client, because she wanted to tell him something. If you have young children at home, unexpected interruptions are inevitable. However, the separation of work and family life becomes easier to understand as children become older.

It is helpful if your at-home work space is completely separate from your family living space so that psychologically you are "at work" rather than "at home." Of course you will blur those boundaries if your children see you wandering into the kitchen for a drink or a snack at odd moments! Many parents who work at home find that their productive work hours are when their children are at school or asleep at night.

Creating an ADD-Friendly Work Space at Home

Having a "Dedicated" Work Space Helps You Dedicate Yourself to Work!

If possible, have an office space at home that is not used for other purposes by other family members. One of the huge advantages of working independently at home as a telecommuter or working for yourself is that you have the opportunity to create an ADD-friendly work space for yourself. Some may have the good fortune to have a very private, separate work space at home, while others may have to creatively devise this space. Be careful, however, not to shortchange yourself. You will need a separate, closed-off space dedicated to your work and organized to suit your work, even if it means giving up a dining room or guest room to create an office. This dedicated space is essential to reduce distractions and to help keep you focused and organized. Using a space dedicated to work helps to give you an "at work" mind-set that you aren't likely to have sitting at the kitchen table.

Set Up Your Telephone System to *Reduce* Distractions, Not Cause Them!

Use an answering machine or answering service to take calls and record messages. Then check your messages and return calls in blocks of time rather than allowing others to randomly interrupt your work-day and break your concentration. If you use an answering machine, don't leave the sound on to screen your calls. This will be a big distraction as you stop your work to listen. If there are people who need to have direct, immediate contact with you, a good system is to have an "inside line" that only they have access to. Others should call you on your "published" work number, leaving you a message to return at your convenience.

Another approach is to place a message on your answering machine that states that you will be available for direct phone calls between certain hours, giving callers the option to leave a message or to call back during your "telephone hour."

A Clear Desk Leads to Clear Thinking!

Clutter management. A clear desk greatly enhances your ability to focus and to sustain your concentration. In fact, serene, uncluttered surroundings in your entire work space will enhance your effectiveness. Even if you are not successful in keeping up with your filing, try to arrange your office space so that your "piles" are not on your desk and are not in your immediate line of vision as you work. Some people find that a credenza placed to the side, or better yet, behind their desk chair can serve this purpose. On the credenza (or shelf) you can place baskets for "action items," such as items "to file," or items "to mail," leaving your desk clear except for the materials you are currently using.

12 ALTERNATIVE JOBS

If You Can't *Use* Your Filing System, You Don't *Have* One!

Filing systems. Many adults with ADD working at home find that developing and maintaining a filing system is one of the most impossible tasks they face. Often they are prone to develop a very detailed filing system, which they don't use consistently. Some adults with ADD report that they have created duplicate files with slightly differing names because they have not developed a simple, logical filing system. Remember, if you don't use your filing system, you don't have a filing system!

While everyone must develop a system that works for them, a general guideline to keeping up with your filing is to make your system very simple. It is far better to have a few large categories of files than to have detailed files that are underused as unfiled papers pile up on every horizontal surface in your office. One man with ADD developed an almost primitive filing system that worked well for him. He purchased a series of square plastic containers, the type sold in discount stores for storing toys, clothing, and the like. He wrote large labels on each, which pertained to some large project or some large aspect of his work, and then literally tossed papers into these storage containers that were lined up on a shelf across one wall of his office. He might have had to do a little searching within each basket to find a particular document, but at least he had created a system simple enough to guarantee that the paper would be somewhere in that particular pile, rather than somewhere in one of any number of piles of unfiled papers.

A Pleasant, Soothing Work Environment Enhances Productivity.

Create a pleasant, soothing, but nondistracting work space. While most of us have little control over our work environment when we are employed by someone else, we have many more degrees of latitude when we create a work space for ourselves at home. It is important to put some thought into arranging your work space to best meet your needs. Many individuals find that they work better when they are exposed to natural sunlight. Place your desk near a window. If you are prone to distract yourself by looking out the window, place your chair facing away from the window but still near it to enjoy the benefit of sunlight.

Think about what colors you would like to be surrounded by and what photographs, pictures, and artwork will give you a feeling of well-being as you work. Do you work well with soft music in the background? If so, invest in a radio or CD player with decent sound quality. One man with ADD who worked at home part-time as a fiction writer found that he worked best listening to rock music at high volume! As a self-employed writer, he was free to accommodate himself in a way that would never be tolerated in a work space shared by others!

Don't Allow Physical Discomfort to Distract You.

Invest in a comfortable chair. You'll be spending a considerable amount of time sitting in it. Make sure, if you write at a computer, that your keyboard is at keyboard height and not desk height. Spending hours holding your hands and arms several inches too high can lead to muscle tension and neck and shoulder problems.

In general, the more ADD-friendly your work space is, the more productive you are likely to be.

Conclusion

B y working independently, whether as a telecommuter, consultant, artist, or businessperson, adults with ADD have the greatest opportunity to custom design their work life. First, try to make an accurate self-assessment. In the numerous ADD stories contained in this chapter, some individuals were very successful in choosing a line of work they loved and in setting up a work environment in which they could function well; others found themselves barely able to function when they were completely on their own. If you are working at home, but struggling with disorganization and procrastination, you may be able to make good use of some of the techniques suggested in this chapter for getting and staying on track. After an honest self-examination, you may decide that, like it or not, you function better as an employee in a more structured job. This book presents you with a wide range of options, both in the office environment and in the home environment. The important thing is to find the levels of stimulation, variety, and autonomy that work best for you.

IN
THIS
CHAPTER

This chapter discusses general issues for women with ADD as well as the impact that some of those issues have on their functioning in the workplace.

13

Women with ADD in the Workplace

U ntil recently, ADD had been considered an almost strictly male disorder. Not only have we come to recognize that ADD is a disorder affecting adults, but we are learning that it affects many more women than was previously thought. As more women are diagnosed, our understanding of ADD may undergo some important changes. ADD has always been viewed through a gender-biased lens owing to the predominantly male population that has been studied. As more women are identified and studied, we may begin to give greater emphasis to other symptoms and may, indeed, even recognize differences in ADD symptom patterns found in men and women.

How Is ADD Different in Women?

Gender Bias in ADD Symptom List?

Many functions and abilities are more highly valued by society for one gender than for the other. For example, being poorly coordinated has a much greater impact on the developing self-concept of a boy than of a girl. A poorly coordinated boy suffers embarrassment, feelings of inadequacy, and perhaps even intense shame. The self-concept of a girl is much less affected by poor coordination since this characteristic is not closely bound to societal expectations and values for females.

Because we have been studying males with ADD, we may very well have ignored ADD patterns that are less important to male than to female functioning. As we begin to diagnose and study more girls and women with ADD, the behaviors of greater concern to them that are affected by the disorder are receiving greater attention. These include verbal skills and other social skills, which may have greater impact on women than on men in terms of both their own needs and society's expectations.

Gender Bias in Response to ADD Patterns of Behavior

Messiness, lack of interest in school, disorganization, impulsivity, risk-taking behavior, and defiance are often associated with ADD—as well as with male adolescents, in whom such behaviors are tolerated and in some cases even admired. Female adolescents who behave in similar ways receive stronger social disapproval from parents, teachers, and peers. For this reason, having ADD of the hyperactive-impulsive type can be a more shameful and destructive experience for a woman than for a man.[1]

Effects of Sex Role Expectations on ADD

Another area that sorely needs study is the way ADD affects a woman's ability to fulfill the demanding social roles expected of her as wife, mother, and household manager, often in addition to full-time breadwinner.

Effects of Male–Female Physiological Differences on ADD

Physiological differences, both neurological and hormonal, between men and women surely affect ADD patterns as well and deserve careful investigation.

At this point, however, we are at the early stages of recognizing that girls and women with ADD exist in larger numbers than ever imagined. The issues described and discussed here are based on my own clinical experience as well as on the clinical experience of others, where noted.

An Example of ADD Gender Bias

In certain workplace situations ADD symptoms may have a much greater impact on women than on men because of the differences in social roles and societal expectations. For example, the job of full-time mother and housewife is one of the most ADD-unfriendly because it provides little structure and involves complex multitasking; frequent interruptions; few breaks; and many routine, boring, repetitive tasks. In contrast to the "ADD unfriendly" job of housewife, positions which provide private offices, structured job requirements, interesting, challenging work, and support staff tend to be much more ADD-friendly. Historically, however, jobs such as these are more likely to be held by a male.

> *Col. and Mrs. MacAndrews were both diagnosed with ADD following the diagnosis of their teenage son. Col. Mc.A. was a military officer of high intelligence. He was opinionated, short-tempered, blunt, argumentative, impatient, and sure of himself (a good example of how a list of ADD traits can, in certain circumstances, be a list of admired male attributes!). He was also surrounded by a squadron of lower-ranking people at his beck and call.*
>
> *As a result of his dominating personality and intelligence, supported by others who could compensate for his ADD, Col. Mc.A. had risen through the ranks of the military. His aides read and summarized reports, minimizing his ADD difficulty*

13 WOMEN

> *(story continued)*
>
> with concentration while reading. Since his dictated letters were typed by his secretary, his own careless errors and misspellings were nowhere in evidence. Mrs. Mc.A. reported that her husband often had no pocket change, usually borrowed money for lunch, and frequently forgot to put gas in the car. His aides were quite used to his habits and covered for him. His energy, intelligence, and strong will got him where he was, and the structure and hierarchy of the military helped cover his ADD dysfunctions.
>
> Mrs. Mc.A. by contrast, had no such support system. In fact, as is true of the majority of women, she was expected to be the family support system. While Col. Mc.A. was feared and revered, Mrs. Mc.A. was seen as the family "flake." Her disorganization, forgetfulness, and emotional reactivity negatively affected everyone in the family. Whereas Col. Mc.A. was too important to be bothered with details like picking up the dry cleaning and remembering the kids' dental appointments, Mrs. Mc.A. was expected to attend to multiple detailed tasks as part of her "job" as wife and mother.
>
> Thus, Col. Mc.A., in spite of his ADD, had a successful career and was viewed as brilliant, dynamic, and forceful whereas Mrs. Mc.A., because of her ADD, was viewed as a generally poor housekeeper and as disorganized, unstable, and ineffective in disciplining her children.

ADD symptoms are always viewed within a context. One context can compensate for ADD symptoms while another can exacerbate them. The contexts in which the Mc.A.'s functioned were profoundly influenced by gender-based expectations and biases.

How Do Women's Roles Interact with ADD in the Workplace?

On the job, women are often expected to play a workplace version of the wife. This supportive role is currently called "administrative assistant" and was formerly called "secretary." While men at work are advised to compensate for ADD symptoms, whenever possible, by relegating responsibilities for details and paperwork to a support person, all too often a woman with ADD does not have this option. In fact, she may be expected to *be* that support person.[2]

Many of the tactics recommended in Chapter 3 to improve job performance can only be applied by people who are self-employed, who have a support person, or who do much of their work independently from others. These coping skills are not typically within the realm of possibility for women who work as secretaries, office managers, teachers, nurses, dental assistants, or administrative assistants!

Multitasking—having to juggle multiple responsibilities while paying attention to detail, particularly in situations where one is frequently interrupted—poses particular difficulty for both men and women with ADD. However, while men in many types of positions may be able to reduce such demands, these are the very tasks that constitute the bulk of the work done by support people—who are often women.

Juggling Home and Work Responsibilities

Men often have ADD coping tactics available to them on the home front, just as they do at work, tactics that are not available to many women. Many men with ADD depend on a non-ADD spouse to be social secretary, homemaker, primary parent, and family organizer and expect her to take responsibility for maintaining and managing, in ways both large and small, the household. These wives often report that their ADD husbands are typically late, cannot be expected to remember important events in the lives of their children, and experience such overload at work that they forget to make phone calls or run errands on their way to or from work.

All of this changes, however, when it is the wife rather than the husband who has ADD. A wife with ADD cannot afford to let things slide at home; if mom is a couch potato after work, the family system rapidly falls apart because meals are not prepared, soccer practice is missed, and the kids are unkempt and undisciplined. Men have been slow to change their role expectations in response to their wives entering the workforce, although there are certainly visible differences between the young fathers of the '90s and those of a generation earlier.

A generation of women in the United States are experiencing frustration and at times sheer exhaustion as they try to perform the functions of full-time homemaker and mother while simultaneously working full time. When ADD is an added factor, a woman's stress level can be tremendous and can have a huge impact on her workplace functioning. A recently published book on women and ADD by Sari Solden[3] focuses on these issues and encourages women with ADD to realistically recognize and accept their limitations rather than continually see themselves as inadequate as they try—and repeatedly fail—to keep all the balls in the air at the same time.

Going to Work May Be Easier Than Staying Home!

In spite of the tremendous stress of being a working woman, a mother, and a household manager, some women with ADD actually experience enormous relief by going to work! This is certainly not true for all jobs, but in some positions women experience a greater ease of functioning because the distractions and interruptions are fewer and the responsibilities are more defined and limited at work than at home.

Naomi, the mother of two school-age children, worked in a professional position reviewing grant proposals, a job she found rewarding. Naomi's ADD crisis occurred when ADD was diagnosed in first one and then the other of her two children. Given their need for treatment, tutoring, and structure, Naomi decided that it would be best to quit her job and focus her time and energy at home. Six months after that decision, she found that she felt she was falling apart. Recognizing many of the same symptoms in herself that she saw in her children, Naomi sought an evaluation; she, too, was diagnosed with ADD.

In her previous lifestyle Naomi's moderate ADD symptoms had been well managed owing to a quiet, orderly daytime routine and reasonable support with household responsibilities. In her new life as full-time homemaker, her ADD symptoms were intensified. Suddenly, her days had little structure. Not earning any income, she now felt obliged to do all of the housework and to cook all the family meals (rather than spending extra money on prepared or carry-out food). She was around her children without the support of her husband many more hours during the week and found that with their noise, arguments, and interruptions she was less and less efficient.

After understanding her ADD symptoms and the structure and supports she needed, Naomi decided to return to her former position. The family soon regained its equilibrium, and Naomi's self-esteem returned once she found herself back in an environment in which she could function effectively.

13 WOMEN

Playing the Support Role at Work

Having ADD doesn't mean that you cannot effectively function in a support staff position, but it does mean that you need to be aware of how you are affected by ADD and that you will need to learn effective ways to compensate for your ADD symptoms. Here are two stories of women with ADD in administrative assistant positions. One decided to leave her position; the other learned ways to successfully compensate and became very effective in her role.

Female Administrative Assistant with ADD: A Bad Match

> *Irene was employed as the administrative assistant to a highly placed boss. The boss was a woman whose judgment, people skills, and grasp of the big picture were excellent. She needed an administrator who could handle details for her, manage her schedule, protect her from unnecessary interruptions, and diplomatically fend off nonurgent phone calls. Irene, although smart and highly motivated, was severely affected by ADD. She had chronic problems with timeliness, was frequently confused when trying to recall names and dates, and responded with frustration to the visitors and phone calls she was forced to deal with as the administrative assistant. In response to the frustration she felt with demands and interruptions, Irene tended to make unilateral decisions to improve the efficiency of the office. These decisions were made with good intentions but with little consideration of the effect they would have on her boss or on the other people who worked under her boss.*
>
> *As tension built between her boss and her, Irene sought ADD-related career counseling. The Myers-Briggs Type Indicator (MBTI; see Chapter 3) revealed that Irene's ADD problems with time management, memory, and organization were not the only cause of her difficulty. The MBTI results suggested that Irene was not cut out to be in a caretaker position. She tended to be impatient and somewhat abrupt and was*

> *(story continued)*
> more concerned with results than with the effects of her actions on others.
>
> Because of the combination of her fairly marked ADD symptoms and her personality type, Irene decided to transfer within her organization to a position much better suited to her traits and talents. With her gain in self-understanding through her ADD counseling, Irene considered this transfer to a new position to be a positive career change rather than a sign of failure in her former position.

Female Administrative Assistant with ADD: A Good Match

> Marge, a woman with ADD, was hired for a position as an administrative assistant in a large organization. She was aware of her problems with planning and organization, which were similar to Irene's, but was able to cope with them in a more effective fashion. Although she, too, had an ADD tendency toward poor time management, she went to extraordinary lengths to always arrive at work on time, or even early. When she realized she was having organizational difficulties, she talked to her boss before the problems became catastrophic. Her boss, sensing her very real motivation, offered to send her to a series of courses on time management and organizational skills. The courses turned out to be very helpful to Marge. Most important, however, were her people skills. Marge genuinely liked interacting with people, both on the phone and in person. Her professional style and her warm manner went a long way to make up for her occasional forgetfulness and her struggles to keep up with the flow of paperwork.

Both Marge and Irene were troubled by ADD symptoms that were incompatible with their job requirements. The differences in their situations had to do with how well their personality types matched their job descriptions. Even without ADD, Irene would have continued to feel frustrated in her position whereas Marge found her contact with people and her helping role very fulfilling.

Having a Support Person at Work

Women with ADD often find themselves in a support position in the workplace. The great majority of women never reach the level of authority in an organization where they enjoy the privilege of having a support person.

> Mary was an attractive, well-dressed, middle-aged woman who had gone back to school in midlife to earn a law degree. She had worked at home as a housewife and mother for many years, a job that she had managed fairly well but that had never fully satisfied her. Mary found, to her delight, that school was a "piece of cake" compared to the responsibilities of husband, home, and children. She graduated with honors and was offered an interesting job as legal counsel for a large nonprofit organization.
>
> Although she had done well in law school, Mary found that in her new position, with its multiple demands and unclear structure, she was having trouble staying organized and focused. To her dismay, her first performance review emphasized her difficulties with planning and organization.
>
> When her son was diagnosed with ADD in college, Mary recognized many of the same patterns in herself. After her initial performance review at work, she was spurred to seek her own evaluation for ADD. Through an assessment she learned

(story continued)

that her hunch was correct. Although medication was pre-
scribed for her ADD, which she found helpful, her biggest
improvement at work resulted from her own detailed analysis of
her job difficulties and in a reconsideration of the duties per-
formed by her half-time administrative assistant.

In counseling, Mary was able to pinpoint the types of
activities that caused her the most difficulty—keeping track of
deadlines, paperwork requirements, and juggling a compli-
cated schedule of meetings and travel. She was able to work out
a new distribution of tasks between herself and her half-time
assistant. The scheduling and coordinating tasks were given to
the assistant, leaving Mary free to do the things she did well and
enabling her to stay on track.

Premenstrual Syndrome and ADD

Another stress that women with ADD face on the job is related to hormonal shifts.[4] While many women struggle with symptoms of premenstrual syndrome (PMS), for example, hypersensitivity, irritability, and hyperemotionality, those with ADD often experience more extreme distress. ADD is the result of a dysregulated neurochemical system. When that dysregulation combines with and interacts with a dysregulated hormonal system each month, the symptoms of each can be exacerbated.

What does this mean for women with ADD in the workplace? First of all, instead of feeling victimized by the ADD-PMS interaction, women should actively seek treatment for both. Many women with ADD have found that it is helpful to take antidepressant medication and to increase the dosage of that medication prior to their PMS time each month. There are many approaches to managing PMS, including rest, diet, vitamins, and certain medications. None of them are foolproof, but all should be considered. Just as ADD needs to be managed rather than suffered from, so too does PMS.

Secondly, women with ADD who experience intense PMS symptoms should plan ahead and avoid, as much as possible, extra stress or heavy commitments during those several days each month when they have the most severe reaction.

Interpersonal Issues at Work

Interpersonal issues at work can sometimes be more difficult for women with ADD than for their male counterparts for several reasons. A number of traits associated with ADD—being assertive, independent, impatient, and inclined to interrupt; having a tendency to take risks—are traits that are more commonly considered masculine. When a man exhibits these traits, he may be viewed as strong or gutsy; unfortunately, these same traits are far less tolerated in women.

Women are expected to be more socially adept, persuasive, diplomatic, sensitive, and responsive. Studies have shown that girls with ADD tend to suffer more interpersonal distress than boys with ADD. There is an expectation that girls will be more verbally adept from a very early age. Social IQ is expected in girls and women; when this is lacking owing to ADD (see Chapter 4, Social Skills), they are less able to fulfill their social role expectations.

Women are raised to fit in, to be accepted by, and to belong to a group of peers. Interpersonal relationships, friendships, and work relationships are more essential, on average, to women than to men. It is not unusual for a man to have few close friends; on the other hand, this state of affairs is unusual for a woman. As a result, women with ADD who have limited social skills suffer more self-doubt, self-recrimination, and unhappiness than do men with the same ADD symptom.

In her book *Women with Attention Deficit Disorder*, Sari Solden describes another typical interpersonal problem experienced by women in the workplace. She finds that they commonly have difficulty in setting limits with others and in asking for the assistance and accommodations they need. Here again, the social conditioning that all female members of our society receive—to be pleasing to others and to place oneself last—takes an especially difficult toll on women with ADD, whose need to be self-nurturing is even greater than that of other women.

These social and interpersonal issues for women with ADD may have important treatment implications that have been overlooked. It may be much more important for women with ADD than for men with this disorder to focus their therapy on developing social skills, assertiveness, and self-acceptance and on finding a more ADD-friendly, accepting group of people to work among.

Conclusion

To summarize, women with ADD in the workplace face a number of challenges that differ from those of men:

- They are typically relegated to the very jobs that are most difficult for people with ADD—detail-oriented support jobs.
- They typically must simultaneously meet the tremendous combined responsibilities of work, home, and children.
- They are placed under different, and in some ways more demanding, social expectations at work.
- Their ADD traits may be seen in a more negative light than those of men.
- Many women with ADD struggle with the additional disequilibrium brought on by premenstrual syndrome.

Given the importance of relationships and interpersonal communication, it may be even more critical for women than for men to find a work situation that is supportive, friendly, encouraging, and non-conflictual. Women with ADD need to become more conscious of the social and emotional demands placed on them both at home and at

13 WOMEN

work and to seek jobs that are less stressful and demanding. This may mean looking for work outside the support and caretaker roles that women have traditionally filled in the past.

Not enough attention has yet been paid to the unique problems of women with ADD. With increased recognition of their differences from men with ADD—socially, emotionally, and physiologically—we may begin to discover better ways to assist women with ADD to improve their functioning in the workplace.

This chapter deals with your legal rights as an adult with ADD and addresses the often asked question "Should I disclose my ADD to my employer?"

ADD and the
Americans with Disabilities Act

A law, pertinent to adults with ADD, is the Americans with Disabilities Act (ADA). This law requires that employers of more than 15 employees give employees whose disabilities are documented certain "reasonable accommodations" in order to allow them to perform their work. It also prohibits discrimination against persons on the basis of their disability. This chapter discusses the ADA, what your rights are, and when you should choose, as a last resort, to engage the services of an attorney if you feel that the law has not been adhered to.

Before any laws can be applied to you as an adult with ADD, you must first inform your employer that you have a disability called Attention Deficit Disorder. The decision to inform an employer is an important one, which we will discuss before going on to outline how the ADA protects adults with ADD in the workplace.

Disclosing Your Disability

In order to officially request accommodations at work on the basis of your disability you must disclose your disability, document your disability, and describe your needs for accommodation.

14 ADD AND THE ADA

Some people feel they are being dishonest by not disclosing a disability during a job interview, but you are not required to do so. In fact, it is illegal for a prospective employer to ask about the presence of disability during a job interview. Furthermore, you have no way of knowing how a potential employer might react to such a disclosure. By disclosing, you will almost certainly take yourself out of the running for the job even if you, with reasonable accommodations, would be an excellent choice for it. The employer certainly does not feel obligated to inform you of all the reasons you might not want to accept the job. Neither are you obligated to inform prospective employers of all the reasons they might have for hesitating to hire you. In an interview, both the potential employer and employee are presenting their best selves.

Generally, disclosure is recommended only when other efforts have failed.[1] Why? Because ADD is an invisible disability that is poorly understood and often interpreted negatively by employers. If you are having difficulty functioning on the job and then decide to disclose your ADD, you run the risk of being seen in an even more negative light. If you are functioning relatively well on the job but choose to disclose your disability, you may bring about subtle, or not so subtle, changes in the way your coworkers view you. This is not always the case. Some people with ADD who choose to disclose receive a helpful response. Thus, you must carefully examine the situation, weighing the pros and cons, before you decide whether or not to disclose.

Positive Disclosure Experiences

Margaret had difficulty with her immediate supervisor but had developed a warm rapport with her department chief. After repeated attempts to request minor and quite reasonable accommodations from her supervisor, Margaret decided to talk with the chief. She disclosed her ADD with some trepidation. As luck would have it, the chief responded very supportively, relat-

(story continued)
ing in confidence that he was a learning disabled adult him-
self. He then worked on Margaret's behalf to influence her
supervisor to provide the support she needed on the job.

Negative Disclosure Experiences

In a group discussion at a recent adult ADD gathering,
Joe related his story almost tearfully, warning others to think
twice about disclosing their ADD.

Joe was a high-ranking executive in a large national cor-
poration when he, along with other managers, was invited to go
on a weekend-long executive retreat. Led by a psychologist,
group members were encouraged to take personal risks in self-
disclosure as an exercise in team building. Joe, entering into the
spirit of the occasion, disclosed that he had never been a good
student and had only barely graduated from college years
before. Working among men who had gone to top colleges, some
of whom had gone on to earn graduate degrees in business and
law, Joe had never before shared this information about his aca-
demic failures. He then went on to disclose that after his son was
diagnosed with ADD, he realized that he had struggled with this
disorder all his life. Finally, he disclosed that he was now receiv-
ing treatment for ADD.

Joe was treated and perceived differently almost imme-
diately after the weekend experience. His boss requested an indi-
vidual meeting to hear more about his ADD. From that time on,
Joe felt that he was gradually shifted out of a position of respon-
sibility. Later, when the company "downsized," Joe was selected
to be laid off. Although his suspicions were difficult to docu-
ment, Joe felt strongly that his being laid off was a direct result

> *(story continued)*
> *of his disclosure during the retreat. Prior to disclosure, he had*
> *an excellent work record and had received a series of promo-*
> *tions; following his disclosure, his influence and authority were*
> *gradually reduced.*

Studies are sorely needed on the outcome experienced by people who choose to disclose their ADD at work. At this point, given general public ignorance about ADD, especially in adults, it seems reasonable to take a cautious approach and to consider disclosure only when all other avenues have been explored and found lacking.

Alternatives to Disclosure

You don't need to discuss your ADD in order to ask for reasonable accommodations. Rather than describing your disorder in terms of a disability that needs accommodations, you can just as easily characterize it as a problem that has possible solutions. In this way, you can present yourself in a positive light—as an employee who is trying to become more efficient at work and is seeking support in doing so.

**Talk about
problems and solutions
rather than
disability and accommodations.**

It may be helpful to refer back to Chapter 3, which describes ways to take charge of ADD patterns at work; there you will find numerous "solutions" that may be useful to suggest to your supervisor.

When You Should Disclose

In spite of negative experiences like those described earlier in this chapter, there are nevertheless circumstances under which disclosure is warranted.

❶ **You should consider disclosing when you feel you will be met by a supportive reaction.** Some fortunate individuals have excellent rapport with their supervisors and feel confident that their value to the firm is well established. If you need accommodations that are unusual enough to require an ADD disclosure in order to explain your request, this may be an appropriate move.

❷ **You should also disclose when all other avenues have been exhausted** and you fear losing your job if you are not granted the accommodations you need to help you adapt to changes in the organization or in your job description. If your reasonable, informal requests for accommodations have all met with resistance, and your ADD symptoms seem to be worsening under the stress of changes in the organization or in your job, then disclosure may be your best option.

❸ **Finally, you should disclose when you are in danger of losing your job because of poor performance.** In such a case, a disclosure may at least buy you some time. Your employer already has a negative impression. It is possible that the ADD disclosure may help him or her understand the performance problems you have been demonstrating. No corporation wants to deal with a discrimination suit if they can avoid it. It is much easier for them to go along with your disclosure and your request for reasonable accommodations. They may fire you later, however, after demonstrating that they provided accommodations and your performance remained unsatisfactory. On the other hand, if the accommodations are part of an overall treatment program in which your performance markedly improves, they may be happy to keep you on.

Your Rights under the Law

The preceding section of this chapter has dealt with whether or not to inform your employer that you have a disability. This section explains briefly exactly how you are legally protected in the workplace as a person with a disability.

Legal Protection under the Americans with Disabilities Act

The Americans with Disabilities Act (ADA) outlaws discrimination against people with disabilities, whether they are employed in the private or public sector (and even extends to people employed by Congress). There are other laws that also pertain to persons with disabilities but the ADA is by far the most important for workplace issues. More detailed information about the ADA and other laws can be found in *Succeeding in the Workplace*, edited by Peter and Patricia Latham (see reference section).

Qualifications for Protection under the ADA[2]

In order to be protected by the ADA in a job discrimination case, you must be able to demonstrate the following:

❶ You have a disability.

❷ You are "otherwise qualified" to perform the job.

❸ You were denied a job or some benefit by reason of your disability.

❹ The employer is covered under the ADA.

Let's explore each of these points in detail.

What Qualifies as a Disability under the ADA?

A disability is a physical or mental impairment that substantially limits one or more of a person's major life functions. Some disabilities, such as blindness and deafness, are self-evident. "Invisible" disabilities like ADD must normally be officially diagnosed by an expert in the field. The expert must provide written documentation of the disability and describe the impairment caused by it. Some employers require both a letter from a physician and a psychological testing report as documentation.

"Otherwise Qualified"

The phrase "otherwise qualified" is critical. You must prove that you are "otherwise qualified" to do the job. That is, you have all of the education, experience, know-how, and ability to do the job and would be entirely able to perform the functions involved if you were given certain specified accommodations. There have been cases in which an employer has claimed that the disability itself disqualifies the person to do the job, and this contention has held up in court.

In cases of physical disability, as compared to those involving attentional or learning problems, it is often easier to see how the disabled person can be accommodated in such a way that he or she can perform the job. Moreover, some cases of ADD affect a majority of areas of functioning, which makes it much more difficult to demonstrate that a person's problems in performing the job would be eliminated if he or she were given certain accommodations.

Denial Strictly on the Basis of Disability

You must be able to demonstrate that your disability was the sole or primary reason you were not selected for the job. An employer is not required to hire you or to retain you because you have a disability! This is an important issue to understand. Some disabled adults, misunderstanding the ADA, believe that they can charge an employer with discrimination solely because they were laid off or were not hired in the first place. Your current or potential employer may have

14 ADD AND THE ADA

a perfectly legitimate reason to prefer someone else over you. Such a preference does not automatically constitute disability discrimination.

Employer Must Be Covered by the ADA

Employers with few employees are not covered by the ADA. This group was excluded because it was felt that the accommodations needed by a person with disabilities would be too costly for a small enterprise. Even in the case of larger enterprises, however, you cannot demand to be granted an unreasonable accommodation (see below).

What Is a Reasonable Accommodation?

A reasonable accommodation is an alteration in the employer's work or testing requirements that would enable an individual with a disability to meet the essential requirements of the job without imposing undue hardship on the employer. Which accommodations are deemed reasonable is generally decided on a case-by-case basis when antidiscrimination suits come to court. Over the course of many such cases, precedents will be established for employers to follow. An organization called Job Accommodations Network (JAN)[3] records and categorizes workplace accommodations for all categories of disabilities. You can request from JAN a list of the types of accommodations that are generally considered reasonable for persons with learning disabilities (ADD is typically lumped together with learned disabilities by the JAN). However, there is no guarantee that you will be granted an accommodation just because it has been listed by JAN. (See Chapter 11 for a list of accommodations, which includes many recommended by JAN.)

Taking Legal Action

You need to think about retaining a lawyer when the following conditions exist:

1 You have requested reasonable accommodations, and those requests have been consistently ignored or denied.

2 Your supervisor has begun creating a "paper trail" in apparent preparation for your dismissal, without giving you the chance to improve your performance with the benefit of necessary accommodations.

3 You feel strongly that your supervisor has a vendetta against you, is purposely denying reasonable requests from you, and is intentionally making your work life unbearable in order to prompt your resignation. (Beware of this one! When you are under great stress, it can be easy to misinterpret actions and attitudes.)

4 Your employer has agreed to provide accommodations but is doing so in a nonaccommodating manner. Designed to cause problems, these accommodations adhere to the letter but not the spirit of the law. Situations like this can arise when a company recognizes that it is required to provide accommodations under the ADA and your supervisor has been instructed by a superior to provide such "accommodations"—for the sole purpose of avoiding a discrimination suit—before dismissing you (or, preferably, prompting your resignation).

Legal action should not be undertaken lightly. Even if you win your case, you should consider what it will be like working for someone whom you have sued. Is this a job you will want? Have you gone through a painful, expensive exercise to vindicate yourself? Is it worth it? Sometimes the answer is "yes." Probably, more often, your money and energies are better spent elsewhere, seeking a different position.

Ron was employed by the federal government as a research scientist. Although a responsible and dedicated employee, Ron suffered, without benefit of diagnosis or treatment, from both ADD and a written language disability. Although Ron was able to do an excellent job as a researcher in the lab, his ADD symptoms and language disability led him to experience enormous difficulty in giving presentations and in writing articles for publication.

Ron was eventually diagnosed with ADD (the learning disability diagnosis came later). He disclosed his ADD diagnosis to his immediate supervisor, from whom he had received poor performance ratings. Moreover, Ron was in jeopardy of losing rank as a senior scientist. Unable to maintain a high output of published papers, required of a scientist of his rank, he was threatened with a demotion to support scientist. Ron, feeling that he had benefited tremendously from his diagnosis and treatment for ADD, requested an opportunity to prove his new capacities before being demoted. However, because of the chronic problems with his supervisor, Ron did not receive the accommodations he had requested for his ADD; furthermore, his supervisor gave him performance requirements that were far beyond the usual, in effect setting him up for failure.

Ron, facing demotion, hired an attorney. An Equal Employment Opportunity Commission (EEOC) hearing was scheduled. All of the events were outlined at the hearing, and the panel decided that Ron had not been given adequate accommodations for his ADD or for his newly diagnosed learning disability. Additionally, the panel found that the requirements placed on Ron to keep his job were unreasonable. Accommodations and a change in requirements were ordered, and Ron was assigned to a more supportive supervisor. In addition, Ron continued to receive counseling for his attentional and learning difficulties and sought the assistance of a tutor to improve his writing skills. His job was saved, and he was able, over the course of the next several months, to clearly meet the job requirements to retain his status as an independent research scientist.

While Ron's story has a happy ending, it is important to emphasize that the process he went through to keep his job was a lengthy, emotionally exhausting one. Furthermore, he was left in the uncomfortable position of continuing to work in association with the man against whom he had defended himself in the EEOC hearings. Such proceedings should only be undertaken as a last resort and only if there seem to be no desirable work alternatives elsewhere.

Negotiating Instead

Instead of bringing a lawsuit against your employer, you might consider negotiating the terms of your departure. Lawsuits are painful and expensive for employers as well as employees. Usually both parties would much rather avoid such an action. If you have a documented disability, feel that you have not received reasonable accommodations made in good faith, and feel that your employer is placing pressure on you to resign, it may be best to talk directly to your supervisor; discuss your grievances, your rights, and your disability; and suggest that a settlement be negotiated prior to your voluntary departure to avoid the pain and expense of a lawsuit for all concerned. In exchange for dropping the lawsuit and leaving voluntarily, you might consider negotiating for the following:

- Employment extended for a specific time period in which you actively seek another job
- Severance pay
- Written letter of recommendation

A satisfactory severance package was won by a man who was himself a lawyer. He had done very productive work for his organization over a number of years. When the administration changed, however, his ADD traits of poor organization and poor time management were much less tolerated by the new regime. This man suspected he had ADD and obtained a diagnosis. He chose to disclose it immediately because his job was already in jeopardy. When it became clear

14 ADD AND THE ADA

to both sides that they faced a nasty battle, the negotiated agreement was a relief to all. Unfortunately, most adults with ADD don't have the leverage to negotiate such a departure.

Conclusion

To summarize, the ADA has given much-needed support in the workplace to persons with disabilities and is leading to improved awareness of and sensitivity to disabled persons at work. The law, as it is written, is broad and general. What accommodations are reasonable for a person with ADD to request of his or her employer has not yet been established.

If things have gone so wrong that you are strongly considering a lawsuit, you should even more strongly consider alternative employment! Bringing a lawsuit against an employer is lengthy and costly. There is no guarantee that you will win the suit, and if you do, there is little likelihood that keeping the job you have fought for will be good for you. There are certainly circumstances in which filing a suit is appropriate, but in the majority of cases the process will be painful and destructive and will take your attention away from making positive changes in your work life. Normally, it is much easier to find a better position than to force an unwilling employer to improve your current one. Don't lose sight of your real objective: finding a workplace where you can grow and thrive.

This final chapter summarizes the information provided in this book and offers a framework for you to build on in creating your own ADD workplace success story.

15

Achieving Success in the Workplace

Making the Career Process ADD-Friendly

This book has covered a tremendous range of material concerning Attention Deficit Disorder in the workplace. At this point you may feel a little overwhelmed, not knowing where or how to begin. You may harbor a secret wish that someone would just identify the perfect job for you so that you could go find it and live happily ever after, without bothering with all of the issues I have discussed in this book. An understandable wish!

Of course you feel overwhelmed! This final chapter offers you something that can help you get started and that you can also use as a model for handling complicated long-term projects: a short summary of the highlights covered in the book.

Take Charge of Your ADD so It Won't Take Charge of You!

Taking charge means becoming an actor rather than a reactor. What is an actor? An actor is someone who sets a course for him- or herself rather than staying in a reactive mode. Many people with ADD have lived their entire lives in a reactive mode, responding to whatever random opportunity or event comes their way. The most important message of this book is that to take charge of your ADD, of your career, and of your life, you need to develop the attitude and skills of an actor.

Actors act on their world; reactors react to their world.

An actor is a problem solver, a solution seeker. ADD actors work to control events inside themselves, by managing their ADD symptoms, and outside of themselves, by finding or creating an ADD-friendly environment. These actors seek ways to work with and to even profit from their ADD rather than allow their ADD to work against them.

Taking charge means managing troublesome ADD patterns. You can't tackle them all at once, and you shouldn't try to tackle them all alone. With the help of a counselor or coach, you can pinpoint your most troublesome ADD patterns, identify which one to work on first, and then problem-solve to find the best management techniques. After you have found the best approaches, don't expect yourself to change overnight. Building new habits takes practice.

Remember the four P's
- **Pinpoint**
- **Prioritize**
- **Problem-solve**
- **Practice**

Don't Approach Habits like a Crash Diet! They Take Time to Develop

Many adults with ADD report that they never really learned how to develop habits as a child. Many adults with ADD treat habit development like a crash diet. They make a resolution, expect perfection of themselves, and quit in defeat a few days or weeks later. A habit takes lots of repetition to develop. Parents have to remind their children hundreds of times to brush their teeth before the children develop the habit. Just as you shouldn't expect a child to develop a new habit overnight, neither should you expect this of yourself. Learning ADD management skills is the process of developing many small habits. Don't despair. Start small, and keep at it (a coach or counselor can help).

Taking Charge Means Understanding Yourself

For real understanding, testing is helpful. Not everyone needs every type of test. At a minimum, you should complete the ADD Workplace Questionnaire in this book, and take the Myers-Briggs Type Indicator. Both are quick and usually inexpensive. Learning disability testing should only be considered if you answered "yes" to a number of items in the section "Related Cognitive Difficulties" in the ADD Workplace Questionnaire. Interest and ability testing can be useful if you don't feel you have a good idea of yourself in these areas. The better you understand yourself, your values, your personality, your talents, your weak points, and your interests, the better the career choice you will make.

Create an ADD-Friendly Environment

Taking charge means finding or creating an ADD-friendly environment. One of the most damaging effects of ADD is the relentless stream of negative feedback received over a lifetime. As an adult you have the chance to look for employers who will enjoy and appreciate your best traits. Look for workplace environments that are not rigid, rule-bound, and focused on details. This doesn't mean that you don't want to change some of your ADD patterns. But having coworkers and supervisors who are impatient, irritated, and frequently critical of your

15 SUCCESS

behavior is not likely to help you make positive changes. By contrast, feeling good about yourself and your accomplishments at work can give you the strength and motivation to work on problem areas more effectively.

Finding people who like and appreciate you is wonderful, but you also need to work toward creating an environment that is truly ADD-friendly. Reading Chapter 9, "An ADD-Friendly Environment" will help you recognize some of the factors to look for.

**Put yourself
where you'll be appreciated!**

Advocate for Yourself at Work

Taking charge means advocating for yourself at work. Set a goal to become an expert on yourself in the workplace. While your employer can provide some accommodations, the responsibility for career success lies with you. Here are some guidelines to follow as you advocate for yourself:

❶ Show that you are motivated to succeed on the job.

❷ Approach problems with a positive attitude.

❸ Be specific in describing your needs to your employer.

❹ Make reasonable requests.

❺ Don't approach the issue of accommodations from an adversarial position but rather from a win–win position.

❻ Don't just focus on what you need or want; demonstrate to your supervisor that you are working hard to overcome problem patterns.

Taking charge means understanding your legal rights.

- Carefully consider the pros and cons of disclosing your ADD.

- Carefully consider the pros and cons of taking legal steps to defend your rights at work.

- Consult an attorney when all other efforts have failed to produce workable results.

- Understand your responsibilities and the responsibilities of your employer under the Americans with Disabilities Act.

Make ADD-Smart Career Choices

Taking charge means making ADD-smart career choices or changes. With the assistance of an ADD expert, learn as much as possible about your strengths, weaknesses, interests, special talents, and ADD needs. Then carefully consider all your options. Ask yourself the following questions:

- Can I make changes in me that will improve my current job?

- Can I make changes in my job that will improve my performance?

- Do I have the right career but the wrong job?

- Do I need to rethink my career?

Conclusion

Y ou can create your own ADD success story by taking charge of your ADD.

Work toward developing a positive, proactive stance toward your work life:

1 Realistically assess your ADD traits, and learn how to manage them.

❷ Understand your interests, abilities, and personality traits.

❸ Recognize and use the positive side of your ADD.

❹ Actively develop ADD success traits.

❺ Actively seek an ADD-friendly work environment.

❻ Become an effective self-advocate at work.

❼ Remember the positive ADD traits found in successful adults.

❽ Appreciate the positive side of your ADD and put it to work for you.

Taking charge means approaching ADD with a positive attitude.

Making the career choices and changes you want will take time and perseverance. You don't need to do it all on your own, and you shouldn't try to do it all at once. By putting into action the steps outlined in this book, you can become your own ADD success story!

Appendix

ADD Workplace Questionnaire

The ADD Workplace Questionnaire has been developed to help you think about the effects of your ADD at work in a systematic fashion. This questionnaire can be used by your therapist or counselor to help you consider issues of workplace functioning. It may be helpful to use this questionnaire with a career counselor if you are in the process of career change.

The ADD Workplace Questionnaire is available separately in an 8½″ × 11″ format. For information and to order see "Rating Scales" on page 237 of the Resources section.

This questionnaire is not a diagnostic tool. It is meant to be used by adults who have already been diagnosed with ADD as a means of pinpointing clusters of problem behaviors in the workplace as a first step toward problem-solving. To be used most effectively, it should be filled out by both you and someone at work who knows you and your work habits well. If you are not comfortable having someone at work complete the questionnaire, it may be helpful to have a spouse, a good friend, or your therapist go over the items with you. Why? Because many adults with ADD are typically inaccurate self-observers. You may be doing things you are unaware of, or you may be doing them to a much greater extent than you realize. As part of the process of self-analysis, which is essential to solving your workplace problems, you need an accurate assessment. Honest feedback, given supportively, by someone you trust can be a valuable piece of this assessment process.

The questionnaire is divided into several sections. In the first section, the questions focus on how ADD traits may affect your capacity to perform your work. In the second section, the focus is on how your ADD traits may affect interpersonal relationships at work. The third section focuses on cognitive issues related to ADD, and the final section focuses on issues in the physical environment of the workplace.

ADD Workplace Questionnaire

Terms such as frequently or very or prone to are open to interpretation. Don't agonize over any one answer. You are searching for patterns and tendencies here. All individuals encounter some of the problems listed below from time to time. This questionnaire is meant to help you pinpoint areas of difficulty at work so that you can begin to problem-solve.

Please rate yourself using the following code:

0—Not at all
1—Slightly
2—Moderately
3—Considerably
4—Extremely

Issues to which you assign a score of 3 or 4 are clearly areas of concern for you. Generally, it is more helpful to look at the score for a cluster of questions than for single scattered questions. Therefore, average your responses in each cluster of questions. If the average is 3 or 4 for any cluster, this may be an area for which you need to actively seek solutions.

ADD Patterns Affecting Work Performance

Inattention/Distractibility

(1) ____ I frequently shift from one activity to another at work.

(2) ____ I am easily distracted by the conversations of coworkers.

③____ My mind wanders when I try to read reports and memos.

④____ It is hard for me to return to a task after an interruption.

⑤____ My best work is done early or late in the workday, when there are few distractions.

⑥____ It is difficult for me to listen consistently during long meetings.

⑦____ I am prone to leave tasks incomplete because I jump to something I forgot to do earlier.

⑧____ It is hard to stay focused on one thing because other ideas intrude.

⑨____ I daydream frequently at work.

Hyperfocusing

①____ I become so involved in one project that I forget about other responsibilities.

②____ When I am really interested in a project, I lose all track of time and can work nonstop for hours.

③____ Sometimes I am oblivious to things occurring around me because I'm so wrapped up in what I'm doing.

Impulsivity

①____ I tend to jump into projects with little planning.

②____ I enthusiastically begin projects but soon lose interest.

③____ I am prone to do things on the spur of the moment, according to my mood.

④____ I typically agree to do something before I consider other commitments.

Hyperactivity/Restlessness

①_____ I feel very restless during meetings.

②_____ I need to doodle or fiddle with small objects during meetings.

③_____ It's hard for me to stay at my desk for long at one stretch.

④_____ I seem to take more breaks than my coworkers because I need to move around.

⑤_____ I tend to tap, fidget, swing my leg, and so on, when sitting.

⑥_____ I prefer work that allows me to move from one job site to another.

⑦_____ I seem to move at a faster pace than the rest of the world.

Need for Stimulation/ Intolerance of Routine

①_____ I become bored very easily.

②_____ I have quit a job simply because I needed something new.

③_____ I am much happier thinking up new ideas than carrying them out.

④_____ I am a "big picture" person who dislikes tending to the details.

⑤_____ When doing detailed work, I am prone to make careless errors.

Memory

①_____ I tend to forget things I have been told.

②_____ If I don't write down information, I'm likely to forget it.

③ _____ I am prone to forget to do what I have promised.

④ _____ I frequently misplace personal items.

⑤ _____ It's hard for me to remember to do something at a particular time.

Time Management

① _____ I am frequently late for work.

② _____ I am often late for meetings during the day.

③ _____ I usually underestimate how much time a task will require.

④ _____ I try to do too many things at once.

⑤ _____ I tend to procrastinate.

⑥ _____ It's hard for me to meet deadlines.

Paperwork

① _____ My desk at work is usually overflowing.

② _____ I am often behind on my paperwork.

③ _____ I tend to make careless errors when doing paperwork.

④ _____ I tend to read things too quickly and to miss important information.

⑤ _____ My filing system is disorganized.

⑥ _____ I am usually behind on my filing.

⑦ _____ I have difficulty keeping accurate records of expenses and activities.

Organization

① _____ I like structure but have difficulty creating it.

② _____ When I try to organize, I'm back to the same old clutter within a few days.

③ _____ I have difficulty in consistently using a day planner to schedule my day.

④ _____ Long-term projects are hard for me to organize.

⑤ _____ I often go through my day without a plan, simply reacting to events.

⑥ _____ I tend to improvise rather than plan in advance.

Interpersonal Stresses Related to ADD Patterns

Many of the patterns listed above affect interpersonal interactions at work. However, the emphasis in the first section of the questionnaire has been on efficacy in performing the job. In this second section, we shift the focus to help you examine how your ADD patterns may affect your ability to get along with and work well with others.

Distractibility

① _____ I have trouble listening consistently when someone is speaking to me.

② _____ I tune out in meetings and may seem uninterested.

③ _____ I tend to avoid interactions with others in order to focus on my work.

Hyperfocusing

① _____ When I'm wrapped up in my work, I sometimes don't hear others when they speak to me.

② _____ Sometimes I'm so involved in my own thoughts that I don't stop to greet or interact with coworkers as I pass them.

③ _____ I am prone to ignore the importance of communicating with others about the work I am doing.

Impulsivity

1 _____ I tend to interrupt others in conversation.

2 _____ Sometimes I say things before thinking of possible consequences.

3 _____ I tend to do things as they occur to me without stopping to consult with my supervisor or coworkers.

4 _____ I may be considered a "loose cannon" at times because of my tendency to react impulsively and unpredictably.

Hyperactivity/Restlessness

1 _____ I may make others uncomfortable by fidgeting or fiddling while listening to them.

2 _____ I become obviously frustrated with the slower pace of others.

3 _____ I am impatient with the lengthy discussions that take place before any decision is made.

4 _____ I dislike just sitting around talking at meetings, giving others the impression their company is not important to me.

Need for Stimulation (Intolerance of Routine)

1 _____ I may irritate others by leaving the details of a job to them.

2 _____ I may appear irresponsible because I like to think up new ideas but rely on others for the follow-through.

3 _____ Hoping that someone else will pick up the ball, I am prone to avoid the routine, boring tasks.

Memory

1 _____ I make promises and then forget to keep them.

②_____ I often forget things people have told me.

③_____ I tend to rely on others to remind me of things.

④_____ I frequently need to borrow items from others because I have forgotten or misplaced my own.

Time Management

①_____ I am frequently late for work.

②_____ I am often late for meetings during the day.

③_____ I tend to keep people waiting because I am running late.

④_____ It's hard for me to meet deadlines others give me.

Paperwork

①_____ If someone needs a paper from me, I typically have difficulty finding it right away.

②_____ I rarely turn in paperwork on time, sometimes making it necessary for others to remind me.

③_____ I tend to skim through memos and letters others write to me, often missing important details contained in them.

Organization

①_____ My disorganization interferes with the ability of my coworkers to work efficiently.

②_____ I have difficulty managing and supervising others.

③_____ I tend to rely on others to provide structure on long-term projects.

Autonomy Issues

①_____ I dislike being closely supervised.

②＿＿＿ I have been described as argumentative.

③＿＿＿ I have been described as stubborn.

④＿＿＿ I tend to keep on and on about something if I think I'm right.

⑤＿＿＿ I am happier working independently than on a team.

Emotional Reactivity

①＿＿＿ I tend to react defensively when criticized.

②＿＿＿ I have low tolerance for frustration.

③＿＿＿ I tend to have strong emotional reactions.

④＿＿＿ I have lost my temper at work.

⑤＿＿＿ I easily become impatient with others.

Emotional Sensitivity

①＿＿＿ My feelings are easily hurt at work.

②＿＿＿ I find it hard to work when there are interpersonal conflicts, even if they don't directly involve me.

③＿＿＿ Having a positive relationship with my supervisor is very important for me.

④＿＿＿ It is hard for me to accept "constructive criticism."

Emotional Insensitivity

①＿＿＿ I am not as tuned in to the feelings of others as I should be.

②＿＿＿ I am prone to make suggestions or comments in a nondiplomatic fashion.

③＿＿＿ I am sometimes unaware that my behavior is upsetting to others.

Related Cognitive Difficulties

The statements in the following list do not refer to official ADD traits but to cognitive difficulties that are often experienced by people with ADD. Answering "yes" to some of these questions may indicate that a learning disability evaluation is in order.

Related Cognitive Problems

① _____ Sometimes I become so mentally exhausted that I can hardly think.

② _____ I seem to take longer than others to learn new material.

③ _____ I have always had problems with spelling.

④ _____ I know what I want to say, but it's hard to put my thoughts in writing.

⑤ _____ It is much easier for me to learn from written than from verbal presentations.

⑥ _____ Reading has always been laborious for me; I would much rather learn by being shown or told than by reading.

⑦ _____ I have difficulty reading maps or following directions to unfamiliar locations.

⑧ _____ Math has always been difficult for me.

Environmental Sensitivities Related to ADD

The following sensitivities are not recognized as ADD symptoms but are often reported by individuals with ADD and need to be recognized and managed.

Sensitivity to the Physical Work Environment

① _____ Fluorescent lights bother me.

② _____ I am very sensitive to noises in the workplace.

③ ____ I am very sensitive to the air temperature at work.

④ ____ It is hard for me to work in a room that has no natural light.

⑤ ____ Unpleasant physical surroundings greatly detract from my ability to work effectively.

⑥ ____ I am very sensitive to crowded work spaces.

How to Use the ADD Workplace Questionnaire

The preceding questionnaire is not a test or diagnostic tool but a structured questionnaire designed to assist you in examining the difficulties you, as an adult with ADD, may experience in the workplace. Don't worry about your score in any particular group of questions. The point of the questionnaire is simply to help you assess your areas of concern so that you can be more effective in seeking solutions to problems. Several chapters in this book are devoted to practical suggestions for managing difficulties in each of these areas.

The most effective way to use the information from the questionnaire is by following these steps:

❶ Identify your problem clusters—those clusters of questions in which you assigned yourself many 3's and 4's.

❷ Rank these clusters in order, starting with the cluster that you feel has the most negative impact on your work performance.

❸ Do not try to tackle everything at once.

❹ Pick a cluster to work on and engage in creative problem solving with yourself, your counselor, and, if appropriate, your supervisor at work. Solutions may involve a number of things including: (1) changing habits on your part; (2) environmental changes, such as a more organized or less distracting work space, and (3) alterations in work patterns or job description to better suit your needs.

References

CHAPTER 1

1 Franklin, B. *Poor Richard's Almanack.*
2 Hartmann, T. (1993). *Attention Deficit Disorder: A Different Perception.* Penn Valley, CA: Underwood-Miller.
3 Children and Adults with Attention Deficit Disorder, 499 NW 70th Ave., Suite 308, Plantation, FL 33317.
4 National Attention Deficit Disorder Association, 9930 Johnnycake Ridge Rd., Mentor, OH 44063.
5 Jaffe, P. (1995). History and overview of adulthood ADD. In K. Nadeau, (Ed.), *A Comprehensive Guide to Attention Deficit Disorder in Adults: Research, Diagnosis, and Treatment.* New York: Brunner/Mazel.
6 See note 5.
7 Hallowell, E., & Ratey, J. (1994). *Driven to Distraction: Recognizing and Coping with Attention Deficit Disorder from Childhood through Adulthood.* New York: Pantheon Books.
8 Individuals with Disabilities Education Act, U.S. Code, vol. 20, secs. 1400 et seq. (1990). (This was formerly known as the Education for All Handicapped Children Act.)
9 Americans with Disabilities Act, U.S. Code, vol. 42, secs. 1201 et seq. (1990).
10 See note 2.
11 See note 2.
12 Dixon, E. (1995). Impact of adult ADD on the family. In K. Nadeau, (Ed.), *A Comprehensive Guide to Attention Deficit Disorder in Adults: Research, Diagnosis, and Treatment.* New York: Brunner/ Mazel.
13 See note 12.
14 Wender, P. (1995). *Attention Deficit Hyperactivity Disorder in Adults.* New York: Oxford University Press.
15 Barkley, R. A. (1993). An update on draft of DSM-IV criteria for ADHD. ADHD Report, 1, 3.
16 Jaffe, P. (1995). ADD as a political football. ADDendum, 18–19.
17 See note 16.

[18]Limbaugh, R. Transcript of 5/5/94 edition of "Rush Limbaugh: The Television Show." Livingston, NJ: Burrelle's Information Services, 1994, pp. 1-3, 11-12.

CHAPTER 2

[1] Kelly, K. & Ramundo, P. (1993). *You Mean I'm Not Lazy, Stupid, or Crazy?!* Cincinnati, OH: Tyrell & Jerem Press.
[2] Hartmann, T. (1994). *Focus Your Energy—Hunting for Success in Business with Attention Deficit Disorder*. New York: Simon & Schuster.
[3] Winter, B. (1993). *Making a Living Without a Job*. New York: Bantam Books.
[4] Sinetar, M. (1987). *Do What You Love, The Money Will Follow*. New York: Dell Publishing.
[5] Berner, J. (1994). *The Joy of Working From Home*. San Francisco, CA: Berrett-Koehler Publishing.
[6] Bolles, R. (1995). *What Color Is Your Parachute?* Berkeley, CA: Ten Speed Press.

CHAPTER 4

[1] Hyatt, C., & Gottlieb, L. (1988). *When Smart People Fail: Rebuilding Yourself for Success*. New York: Viking Penguin.
[2] Ratey, J., Hallowell, E., & Miller, A. (1995). Relationship dilemmas for adults with ADD: The biology of intimacy. In K. Nadeau (Ed.), *A Comprehensive Guide to Attention Deficit Disorder in Adults: Research, Diagnosis, and Treatment*. New York: Brunner/Mazel.
[3] Weiss, L. (1992). *Attention Deficit Disorder in Adults: Practical Help for Sufferers and Their Spouses*. Dallas, TX: Taylor.

CHAPTER 5

[1] Hallowell, E., & Ratey, J. (1995). *Answers to Distraction*. New York: Pantheon.
[2] Sandler, A. (1995). Attention deficits and neurodevelopmental variations in older adolescents and adults. In K. Nadeau (Ed.), *A Comprehensive Guide to Attention Deficit Disorder in Adults: Research, Diagnosis, and Treatment*. New York: Brunner/Mazel.
[3] Latham, P., & Latham, P. (Eds.). (1994). *Succeeding in the Workplace—Attention Deficit Disorder and Learning Disabilities in*

the Workplace: A Guide for Success. Washington, DC: JKL Communications.

[4] Richard, M. (1995). Students with attention deficit disorder in post-secondary education: Issues in identification and accommodation. In K. Nadeau (Ed.), *A Comprehensive Guide to Attention Deficit Disorder in Adults: Research, Diagnosis, and Treatment.* New York: Brunner/Mazel.

[5] See note 3.

CHAPTER 6

[1] Myers, I. B., & Briggs, K. C. (1976). Myers-Briggs Type Indicator. Palo Alto, CA: Consulting Psychologists Press.

[2] Martin, C. (1995). Looking at Type and Careers. Gainesville, FL: Center for Applications of Psychological Type.

[3] Myers, I. B. (1980). *Gifts Differing.* Palo Alto, CA: Consulting Psychologists Press.

[4] Keirsey, D., & Bates, M. (1984). *Please Understand Me: Character and Temperament Types* (3rd ed.). Del Mar, CA: Prometheus Nemesis Books.

[5] See note 4.

[6] See note 4.

[7] See note 4.

[8] Meisgeier, C., Poillion, M., & Haring, K. (1994). The relation between ADHD and Jungian psychological type: Commonality in Jungian psychological type preferences among students with Attention Deficit Hyperactivity Disorder. Proceedings of the international symposium, Orchestrating Change in the 90s: The Role of Psychological Type, Gainesville, FL.

CHAPTER 7

[1] Hartmann, T. (1993). *Attention Deficit Disorder: A Different Perception.* Penn Valley, CA: Underwood-Miller.

[2] Hallowell, E., & Ratey, J. (1994). *Driven to Distraction.* New York: Pantheon.

[3] Hartmann, T. (1994). *Focus Your Energy: Hunting for Success in Business with Attention Deficit Disorder.* New York: Simon & Schuster.

CHAPTER 8

[1] Gerber, P., Ginzberg, R., & Reiff, H. (1992). Identifying alterable patterns in employment success for highly successful adults with learning disabilities. *Journal of Learning Disabilities, 25,* 475–487.

[2] Kelly, K., & Ramundo, P. (1993). *You Mean I'm Not Lazy, Stupid, or Crazy?! A Self-Help Book for Adults with Attention Deficit Disorder.* Cincinnati, OH: Tyrell & Jerem Press.

[3] Hallowell, E., & Ratey, J. (1995). *Answers to Distraction.* New York: Pantheon.

[4] Hartmann, T. (1994). *Focus Your Energy: Hunting for Success in Business with Attention Deficit Disorder.* New York: Simon & Schuster.

CHAPTER 9

[1] Wender, P. (1995). *Attention Deficit Hyperactivity Disorder in Adults.* New York: Oxford University Press.

[2] Kroeger, O., & Thuesen, J. (1992). *Type Talk at Work: How the 16 Personality Types Detetmine Your Success on the Job.* New York: Bantam Dell Doubleday.

[3] Hartmann, T. (1994). Focus Your Energy: *Hunting for Success in Business with Attention Deficit Disorder.* New York: Simon & Schuster.

[4] See note 3.

CHAPTER 11

[1] Job Accommodations Network, a service of the President's Commission on Employment of People with Disabilities, 809 Allen Hall, West Virginia University, Morgantown, WV 26506.

[2] Americans With Disabilities Act, U.S. Code, vol. 42, secs. 12101 et seq (1990).

CHAPTER 12

[1] Winter, B. J. (1993). *Making a Living Without a Job: Winning Ways for Creating Work That You Love.* New York: Bantam Books.

[2] Sinetar, M. (1989). *Do What You Love, the Money Will Follow.* New York: Dell.

[3] See note 1.

[4] Hartmann, T. (1993). *Attention Deficit Disorder: A Different Perception.* Penn Valley, CA: Underwood.

[5] Murphy, E. (1996). *Flexible Work.* Hertfordshire, England: Director Books.

[6] See note 4.

[7] See note 4.

[8] Kelly, K., & Ramundo, P. (1993). *You Mean I'm Not Lazy, Stupid or Crazy?!: A Self-Help Book for Adults with Attention Deficit Disorder.* Cincinatti, OH: Tyrell & Jerem Press. p. 191.

[9] Douglass, M. E., & Douglass, D. N. (1993). *Manage Your Time, Your Work, Yourself.* New York: American Management Association.

CHAPTER 13

[1] Ratey, J., Miller, A., & Nadeau, K. (1995). Special diagnostic and treatment considerations in women with Attention Deficit Disorder. In K. Nadeau (Ed.), *A Comprehensive Guide to Attention Deficit Disorder in Adults: Research, Diagnosis, and Treatment.* New York: Brunner/Mazel.

[2] Hartmann, T. (1994). *Focus Your Energy: Hunting for Success in Business with Attention Deficit Disorder.* New York: Simon & Schuster.

[3] Solden, S. (1995). *Women with Attention Deficit Disorder.* Grass Valley, CA: Underwood Press.

[4] See note 1.

CHAPTER 14

[1] Latham, P., & Latham, P. (Eds.). (1994). *Succeeding in the Workplace.* Washington, DC: JKL Publications.

[2] See note 1.

[3] Job Accommodations Network, a service of the President's Commission on Employment of People with Disabilities, 809 Allen Hall, West Virginia University, Morgantown, WV 26506.

Resources

Rating Scales

The ADD Workplace Questionnaire shown in this book can be ordered separately, in a 12-page 8½″ × 11″ format (Order Number 0-87630-872-8). For information call 1-800-821-8312 (Fax 215-785-5515) or write to Taylor & Francis, 1900 Frost Road, Suite 101, Bristol, PA 19007

Books

Books on ADD

Adventures in Fast Forward: Life, Love, and Work for the ADD Adult. By Kathleen G. Nadeau. New York: Brunner/Mazel, 1996.

A Comprehensive Guide to Attention Deficit Disorder in Adults: Research, Diagnosis, and Treatment. Edited by Kathleen Nadeau. New York: Brunner/Mazel, 1995.

Attention Deficit Hyperactivity Disorder in Adults. By Paul Wender. New York: Oxford University Press, 1995.

Driven to Distraction: Recognizing and Coping with Attention Deficit Disorder from Childhood through Adulthood. By Edward M. Hallowell and John Ratey. New York: Pantheon Books, 1994.

Answers to Distraction. By Edward M. Hallowell and John Ratey. New York: Pantheon Books, 1995.

You Mean I'm Not Lazy, Stupid, or Crazy?! A Self-Help Book for Adults with Attention Deficit Disorder. By Kate Kelly and Peggy Ramundo. New York: Scribner's, 1995.

Women with Attention Deficit Disorder. By Sari Solden. Grass Valley, CA: Underwood Press, 1995.

ADD Success Stories. By Thom Hartmann. Grass Valley, CA: Underwood Press, 1995.

Attention Deficit Disorder in Adults: Practical Help for Sufferers and Their Spouses. By Lynn Weiss. Dallas: Taylor, 1992.

Books Relating to ADD Workplace Issues

Succeeding in the Workplace—Attention Deficit Disorder and Learning Disabilities in the Workplace: A Guide for Success. By

Peter S. Latham and Patricia H. Latham. Washington, DC: JKL Communications, 1994.

Focus Your Energy: Hunting for Success in Business with Attention Deficit Disorder. By Thom Hartmann. New York: Simon & Schuster, 1994.

Attention Deficit Disorder and the Law: A Guide for Advocates. By Peter S. Latham and Patricia H. Latham. Washington, DC: JKL Communications, 1992.

Books on the Myers-Briggs Type Indicator (MBTI)

Type Talk at Work: How the 16 Personality Types Determine Your Success on the Job. By Otto Kroeger with Janet M. Thuesen. New York: Dell, 1992.

Looking at Type and Careers. By Charles Martin. Gainesville, FL: Center for Applications of Psychological Type, 1995.

Please Understand Me: Character and Temperament Types (3rd ed.). By David Keirsey and Marilyn Bates. Del Mar, CA: Prometheus Nemesis Books, 1984.

Books on Educational Issues for Adults with ADD

ADD and the College Student. Edited by Patricia Quinn. New York: Brunner/Mazel, 1994.

Survival Guide for College Students with ADD or LD. By Kathleen G. Nadeau. New York: Brunner/Mazel, 1994.

Books on Career and Workplace

What Color Is Your Parachute? By Richard Bolles. Berkeley, CA: Ten Speed Press, 1995.

The Joy of Working from Home. By Jeff Berner. San Francisco: Berrett-Koehler, 1994.

Do What You Love, the Money Will Follow. By Marsha Sinetar. New York: Dell, 1989.

Making a Living Without a Job: Winning Ways for Creating Work That You Love. By Barbara Winter. New York: Bantam Books, 1993.

Books on Organization and Time Management

Organize Yourself. By Ronni Eisenberg and Kate Kelly. New York: Collier Books, 1986.

How to Get Control of Your Time and Your Life. By Alan Lakein. New York: Signet, 1973.

Streamlining Your Life. By Stephanie Culp. Cincinnati, OH: Writer's Digest Books, 1991.

Procrastination. By Jane Burka and Lenora Yuen. Reading, MA: Addison-Wesley, 1983.

Do it! Let's Get Off Our Buts. By John Roger and Peter McWilliams. Los Angeles: Prelude Press, 1991.

Organizing for the Creative Person. By Dorothy Lehmkuhl and Dolores Cotter Lamping. New York: Crown Trade Paperbacks, 1993.

The Ten Natural Laws of Successful Time and Life Management. By Hyrum W. Smith. New York: Warner Books, 1994.

Commonsense Time Management. By Roy Alexander. New York: American Management Association, 1992.

The Messies Superguide. By Sandra Felton. Old Tappan, NJ: Fleming H. Revell, 1987.

Getting Organized. By Stephanie Winston. New York: Warner Books, 1991.

Books Containing Lists of Resources for Adults with ADD

Resources for People with Attention Deficit Disorder (ADD) and Related Learning Disabilities (LD). By Marcia L. Connor, Director of Employee Development, Wave Technologies International, Inc. Fax: 404-947-0303; voice mail: 800-994-5767, Ext. 5040; Internet: p00350@psilink.com.

Adulthood ADD Lay Bibliography. Compiled by Paul Jaffe. Available from ADDendum, 5041-A Backlick Rd., Annandale, VA 22003.

Adulthood ADD Professional Bibliography. Compiled by Paul Jaffe. Available from ADDendum, 5041-A Backlick Rd., Annandale, VA 22003.

Good resource lists can also be found in the following books:

Driven to Distraction: Recognizing and Coping with Attention Deficit Disorder from Childhood through Adulthood. By Edward M. Hallowell and John Ratey. New York: Pantheon Books, 1994.

You Mean I'm Not Lazy, Stupid, or Crazy?! A Self-Help Book for Adults with Attention Deficit Disorder. By Kate Kelly and Peggy Ramundo. New York: Scribner's, 1995.

Organizations Concerned with ADD and Learning Disabilities

CH.A.D.D. (Children and Adults with Attention Deficit Disorder)
499 NW 70th Avenue
Plantation, FL 33317
305-587-3700

National Attention Deficit Disorder Association (ADDA)
9930 Johnnycake Ridge Road
Mentor, OH 44063
800-487-2282

Adult ADD Association
1225 E. Sunset Drive, Suite 640
Bellingham, WA 98226
206-647-6681

National Center for Law and Learning Disabilities
P.O. Box 368
Cabin John, MD 20818
301-469-8308

Learning Disability Association
    4156 Library Road
    Pittsburgh, PA 15234
    412-341-1515

The National Coaching Network
    P.O. Box 353
    Lafayette Hill, PA 19444
    610-825-4505

Newsletters/Magazines

ADDvance, Magazine for Women with ADD
    4400 East-West Hwy, Suite 816
    Bethesda, MD 20814

Focus
    P.O. Box 972
    Mentor, OH 44060

On-Line Services

For an extensive listing of on-line ADD services, the reader should refer to Resources for People with Attention Deficit Disorder (ADD) and related Learning Disabilities (LD). By Marcia L. Connor, Director of Employee Development, Wave Technologies International, Inc. Fax: 404-947-0303; voice mail: 800-994-5767, ext. 5040; Internet: p00350@psilink.com.

America Online: There is an adult ADD support room where adults with ADD share support and information. For more information, send e-mail to ERICNJB@AOL.COM.

CompuServe: Look up GO ADD. For more information, send e-mail to 70006.101@compuserve.com.

Prodigy: Has adult ADD support groups listed under Support Groups Medical.

There are Internet chat rooms on various topics pertaining to ADD.

RESOURCES

Tapes and Videos

Many adults with ADD may prefer tapes or videos to the printed page.

Videos on adult ADD have been produced by several experts, including Arthur Robbins and Russell Barkley. Information on ordering copies of these can be obtained through the ADD Warehouse. Call 800-233-9273 to request a free catalog. A half-hour video titled Succeeding in the Workplace with ADD and LD is available from

JKL Communications
P.O. Box 40157
Washington, DC 20016

Tapes have also been made of many of the lectures on adult ADD that have been presented at national conferences.

Adult ADD Association Conference (Ann Arbor, 1993 and 1994) tapes may be ordered through

Take Two Recording and Duplicating Services
1155 Rosewood, Suite A
Ann Arbor, MI 41804

Tapes from the National CH.A.D.D. Convention may be ordered through

Cassette Associates
3927 Old Lee Highway
Fairfax, VA 22050
800-545-5583

Tapes from the 1995 ADDA Adult ADD Conference can be ordered from

Repeat Performance
2911 Crabapple Lane
Hobart, IN 46342

Index